For information contact Living Free Publications (800) 258-8589

Library of Congress Card Number: 2023909179

ISBN 978-0-9622094-3-7

I'm 84 And Living In A Time Warp

Table of Contents

Foreword

PART 1

Time Warp

PART 2

FOREWORD

No matter how you approach your senior years, it is going to be a rough road. You are a target for scam artists out there who will try to con you out of every dollar you are lucky enough to still have in your bank account. It is true, these are the golden years—the years when all the gold leaves your pocket and goes to the doctor's new Mercedes, the banker looking to make a bonus off your naiveté, or a friend or family member who can't wait to get their inheritance.

I have traveled to many countries, talked to thousands of people on a personal level, been a guest in hundreds of homes, and have seen an awful lot. Unfortunately, most of what I will share with you is coming from what people shared with me during those visits and from my own personal experience, as I have fallen prey to many scams myself. If I had a book like this when I was younger, I would have navigated my latter years a *whole lot better* and wouldn't have to still be working full time at eighty-four years of age. I know that hindsight is wonderful, but I hope to give you enough foresight that you won't hit those pitfalls that I and thousands of others have experienced. This book, with God's help, will give you the tools to prepare yourself and provide some guidelines as to how to deal with the problems you will face.

When we are younger, we never think about getting old. We look at being elderly like it is so far off, it really doesn't affect me now. We say, "I will deal with it later", but later never really comes until we suddenly reach hat senior stage unprepared. I liken this to riding a horse on an open, well-cared-for field where it is safe to gallop. As we get older, we gallop faster and faster until we suddenly find ourselves in the middle of a prairie dog village. That is, where there is nothing but holes everywhere, doorways for those beautiful little critters to get to their underground homes. Those holes are great for them, but when you hit them full speed on a horse, that horse can step in one of those holes, break a leg, and down you go. Each prairie dog hole becomes your downfall, something you never expected to have to deal with, but there you are. The chapters in this book will deal with one "hole" after another, how to avoid them, and if you get caught unaware, how to navigate your way out of them and stay on your feet.

Some of the problems will be your own fault, the result of your own bad decisions, but many of them won't. When you read about all the stupid mistakes I have made, you may think me the dumbest, most naïve, trusting person you have ever known. If you do, so be it, because I often think of myself as such. But my prayer is that you will learn from my mistakes and avoid many of them yourself. I lived the way most of my family lived, just falling into the same mistakes they made, as most people do with their family. I am learning a little late, but I am learning. I know God forgives me. I just have to learn to forgive myself.

Patricia
May you find blessing
and help in these pages.

Beatrice Lydecker - Hayford

PART ONE

TIME WARP

This may seem like a strange title, but that is exactly what I think of my life. At eighty-four, the world has changed *so* much, sometimes I feel like I have zoomed into another time zone. When I was a child, the safest place for us to be was in school; now it is one of the most dangerous. Most families stayed together, and children were raised in two-parent homes, not two separate parent homes. We could trust adults to care for us, even felt safe to stay out after dark, but today it isn't safe for a child to walk down the street alone, even in the daylight. I remember getting our first phone, which was a party line, and we laughed about Dick Tracy talking into his watch and Buck Rogers going to the moon, but now they are doing it. In just a hundred years we went from horse and buggy, which has been the transportation for centuries to the age of the Jetsons.

People had dignity, and immorality was called just that. Now immorality is the norm for the present generation, and they have lost all sense of personal dignity. Boys were born boys and stayed that way, and girls stayed as girls. We weren't ashamed of our personal identity.

Our parents told us that God made us who we were because He had a special job for us to do, and we could only do that job as the special person He designed us to be. That is even stated in Ephesians 2:10: "For we are

God's handiwork, created in Christ Jesus to do good works, which God prepared in advance for us to do." The Bible says in Psalms 139: 13,14 and 16: "For you created my inmost being, you knit me together in my mother's womb. I praise you because I am fearfully and wonderfully made, your works are wonderful. Your eyes saw my unformed body; all the days ordained for me were written in your book before one of them came to be." Now kids are told God made a mistake, and we must let them change their sex before they even know what sex is. When they do, they are then incapable of doing what it was God formed them to do, and we miss the best of what God made us for. Parents need to teach this fact to their children over and over until the children are confident as to who they are. If they do, then when those who are trying to indoctrinate their child to believe God made a mistake, that child won't be influenced by the lies.

I know I am doing what God created me to do, which would not have happened had I been changed into a male. Where would a child be if either of his or her parents had had a sex change? They wouldn't even be here. Where would our country be if George Washington had been changed into Georgette? I wonder who God would have chosen to bring the Savior into the world if Mary had become Malcolm? What about that child's future of being a parent and possibly having a child that could change the world? We could go on and on about that.

I was so shocked the other day in talking with someone who believes in sex changes (what really amounts to child mutilation), and they didn't even know that a sex change would sterilize the child! Of course it does! You can't place a uterus and ovaries in a boy or create sperm in a girl and make them able to reproduce!

You can change the anatomy, but you can't change your DNA and your basic bone structure. In the depth of every cell in your body and your bone structures, you are still the original sex you were born with. If there should be a body brought to a coroner to try to find out who that body belonged to, that sex change would foul up their ability to identify the body. Say you were a male transitioned to a female with a new female name. They would be looking for a male instead of the new you, and, boy, would that screw up who they are looking for.

I saw a guy who had "become a girl" on *Dr. Phil* who still had the features, voice, and mannerisms common to a male homosexual. There are certain hand and body movements homosexuals do while trying to act like a female—motions and swaying a female would never do. The same with a guy who transitioned to a girl still had the deep male voice and mannerisms of a male homosexual. They don't lose their basic features.

How stupid can the media be when they said a woman in Redmond, Oregon, who was going through a sex change was the first man to have a baby. Are you kidding me? The saddest thing of all was when they reported the story, they were excited and very serious at this new discovery. Talk about fake news. It can't get much worse than that. You can't call a female a man, because she still has a uterus and eggs, something a man will never have! How a person chooses to live as an adult is their right; they have to give account to God someday for their choices, but little kids have no idea the consequences they face. Sadly, many parents don't either.

One caution here: It is now law in some states to allow the DHS to come and remove your child from your home and care if you refuse to allow them to have a sex change when the child asks for one. Your child, who has no idea of the consequences or what it entails, has probably been prompted by their teacher or doctor to believe they were born in the wrong body, and as most people know, you can influence a child to believe anything. The propaganda aimed at our children makes it more important than ever to help them understand fully the reason God made them the way they are, and God doesn't make mistakes. The Bible needs to be an intricate part of your child's education. It is up to parents to make sure their children understand how special they are and the purpose God has for them. Then, when the teacher or doctor tells them differently, they will be grounded in truth and not believe the lies.

When I was a child, we were taught reading, English, science, true world history—before it was rewritten—and math. The teachers focused on our education and left other life skills up to the parents. There were consequences if we didn't learn the material; we didn't pass to the next grade until we did. Today they pass students if they just show up; they don't even need to know the subjects. This is creating a generation of illiterates that can't even make simple change.

The other day a friend went into the store and paid for the item she bought which meant that she had thirty-five cents in change coming back. The cashier couldn't even figure out a quarter and dime equal thirty-five cents, so she counted out three dimes and a nickel. At another place my friend needed $2.50 in change back from her purchase, and the girl had to call the manager to figure out how to do it. The cash register wasn't updated so it couldn't tell her how much change there was coming to the customer. Once she knew the amount, she couldn't even count it out; the manager had to do it. If things don't change, we won't have a literate next generation, so who will run this country? And you think things are bad now.

Don't get me wrong, there are a lot of great things we have today that we didn't have when I was a child, like indoor toilets and baths, improved transportation, many conveniences that used to involve hard labor, like having water when we need it, without hauling it from the well, or a washing machine instead of hand scrubbing our clothes, and on and on it goes.

With the invention of the TV and the computer, knowledge has exploded, but so has evil. We rarely saw kids being bullied in school because the bully had to face their victim, and everyone knew what they were doing. Those people who were bullies were looked down on and shunned. Sadly, social media enables kids to bully someone into committing suicide without facing that person. Because of this, suicide is rampant today in our teens but was almost never heard of when I was young.

If you are wondering where all this craziness is coming from, read Rabbi Jonathan Cahn's book, *The Return of the Gods*. He explains clearly who the demons are and which ones are behind the sexual problems and who are the ones behind the lawless chaos. It is also explained in Luke 11:24—26. We threw God out of our schools, halls of justice and from our homes, gave Madelyn Murray a platform to spew her atheism and opened the door for demons to come in and destroy our country. We are reaping what we allowed.

I was watching a program on TV the other night when an ad came on inviting people to come and join their atheistic society. The man speaking laughed and said, "I'm not afraid of any god who doesn't exist, so come join us." In Psalms 14:1 he is called a fool: "A fool says in his heart, there is no God." I have news for him: he'll believe in God when he steps out of his body. I guarantee you he will, because I have "seen" Hell through the eyes of people who were dying. They became believers pretty fast. It was a wake-up call. Let me tell you a couple of experiences I have had.

I had lived in Los Angeles, California, for many years where I had been involved in the television industry and had built a solid clientele. It was becoming so dangerous for my animals that I finally moved to Oregon City, Oregon, where I found a twenty-acre place in the woods. Unfortunately, in order to make a living, I had to return to Los Angeles once a month to work. I always stayed with my best friends, Bill and Helen, and Helen's mother, Lottie, all of whom were Atheists.

One day I was packing the motor home to head south when Helen called to ask me when I would be there. She informed me that her mother had liver cancer and was in the hospital, and that her mother became terrified every time she started to die. Since I could communicate with nonverbal people, Helen asked if could please come straight to the hospital and find out what her mother was experiencing. I said sure, and as I drove all the way down there, I was praying.

I parked the motor home in the parking lot and headed for the hospital, asking God to remove Helen from the room so I could talk to her mother about Jesus. I knew Helen would interfere if she were there. As I was going up the elevator, God caused Helen to go down and spent just enough time looking for me, that I was able to talk to Lottie.

When I asked Lottie verbally what she was afraid of, she showed me mentally what she was experiencing. She was being drawn into a light that was coming from a big square opening. From that light, she could hear screaming and moaning, and felt terrible pain. She knew she was being drawn into Hell, and she was terrified! Just above her, there was a man standing with two angels of death holding him back so he couldn't stop her. He had tears streaming down his cheeks as he watched her being sucked into Hell.

I then shared with Lottie the message that Jesus loved her and didn't want her to go there. She could stop that journey if she would acknowledge that Jesus is the Son of God who died for her sins and ask Him to forgive her sins and He would. She communicated back that it was too late. I informed her that as long as she was in her body it was not too late. I prayed with her as she accepted Christ as her Savior.

Just as we finished praying, Helen came back into the room. I told her to read her mom Psalm 23 to help her transition. Helen said, "She won't like that, she's an atheist!" to which I replied, "She isn't anymore!" Lottie died peacefully within hours.

A couple of days later, Helen and I were sitting at her table when she asked me what had happened in that hospital room. I shared it with her. She brought out her family album and asked if I would look at some pictures. She wanted to know if the man watching her mother being sucked into Hell might be in her album. Sure enough, I recognized him. It was Helen's grandfather, who apparently was a very godly man.

Helen couldn't deal with the reality that there was a God and Hell is real, so she wouldn't open her heart to the Lord then, but several years later we were again sitting at her table. She had developed cancer and knew she wasn't going to make it. She quietly asked me, "Do you remember that incident about my mother and how she accepted Christ?" I replied that I did. "Well, I want to know that same Jesus. Would you tell me how?"

I was overjoyed to lead her to Christ. She died peacefully a few months later. I am thrilled to know we will be friends again in Heaven. It's very theatrical and sweet to say, "My friend went into the light," but that light isn't always good, as I have learned. You better be heading into the right one. From personal experience I have "seen" several people and animals passing over, and the animals and people who know Christ as Savior don't go into a light. They are met by loved ones.

I have helped several people who were on their death bed find Christ as their Savior. They suddenly realize where they are going, and it becomes a wake-up call. That guy on the TV who was boasting about being an atheist is going to face the same end too, right along with those who are destroying our children and causing destruction.

The rich may have a lot of money and belongings but it won't go with them when they step out of their bodies and face God. Read Luke 12 about the rich man who built bigger and bigger barns to store all his wealth. He was working to get more and more so he could sit back in leisure "someday." God said, "You fool; today your soul will be required of you." The very wealthy are never satisfied, accumulating more and more wealth, and for what? When they step out of their body it will all be left behind for someone else. Read Mark 8:36: "What does it profit a man if he gains the whole world but loses his own soul?" You have to make that decision while you are still in your body because once you leave, it is over—no second chance. The story of Lazarus is a good example of this in Luke 16. It is a parable telling a truth, which is that there is a gap between heaven and Hell that cannot be crossed once you die. Hebrews 9:27: "It is appointed unto man once to die and after that the judgment."

Hell was not made to be an eternal punishment for man; it was designed as a place of eternal punishment for Satan and his fellow fallen angels, or demons. Satan is trying to take as many people with him as he can, and right now he is doing a bang-up job. Is it really worth the chance of spending eternity in Hell because of your pride or greed? Eternity is a long, long time. Are you willing to take that chance?

If you think demons don't exist, let me tell you of two incidents where I "saw" them, one visibly and the other in my mind's eye. The first one occurred in an apartment in New York City. I was a guest of a lady who had a lot of animal-loving friends. She had me stay with her so they could bring their animals over for me to talk to them.

She was some kind of healer, where she had people come in and she would move her hands over them. I am not sure what all she did, but since it was a one-room, rent-controlled flat, she asked me to go over and sit by the window while she "treated" a client. I usually travel with one of my Chihuahuas, as they are such a comfort to me when I am away from home. So I picked up my dog and moved over to the couch by the window.

As she was getting started, I looked up at the window and literally saw a demon coming through the window. To this day, if I were an artist, I could draw that face—it was so ugly. I quietly said, "In the Name of Jesus, you leave," to which it replied, "I can't touch you or your dog, but this is her place and she invited me in. You can't kick me out." It then went across the room and entered her while she worked over the "patient." It was just a face with a kind of mist around it, but the face was real and clear.

Apparently, she was doing some good, as people wouldn't keep coming back time and time again to have her work on their animals. Satan will often do some good, as Second Corinthians 11:14 says, "Satan himself masquerades as an angel of light." He doesn't care how much good he does, as long as he deceives you and gets your soul. After the client left, I tried to talk to her about God and His son, Jesus. She became so irate she nearly threw me out. She never wanted to hear that stuff again. There was incredible hatred spewing from her mouth about God. Was it any wonder, after I saw the demon enter her? I am sure she believes in God now. Sadly, I think, because she is seeing Him from Hell.

Another time I had been watching the television show, *Ghost Whisperer*. I thought it was a neat idea but didn't realize those ideas were entering my subconscious mind. I have done several exorcisms successfully in the past; so when a person asked me to help identify the dark figure that many people had seen going through her house, I agreed. I was thinking it was a man who had lived and died there a few years before. I thought maybe something had happened, and he couldn't leave, so I expressed that idea to the owner of the house.

A couple of hours later that same picture came into my mind, and suddenly it turned toward me and laughed and said, "Ha, ha! I fooled you into thinking you are helping the dead like the *Ghost Whisperer* does." I knew then that it was a demon, because I saw its face and it was ugly. I quickly got back on the phone and told the woman that I was mistaken—it was a demon. She needed to find a local pastor and get it kicked out of her house.

Since she was in Hawaii and I was in Oregon, I was too far away to do it. Before I perform an exorcism, I always fast and pray, as Jesus said in Mark 9:29, "These things only come out by prayer and fasting." Then, when I am finished with the exorcism, I always go through the house and anoint all the doors and windows with oil. I also make sure they have no books or anything from the occult or new age gimmicks like demon-filled Ouija boards, because that just brings them right back in.

I have seen miracles of God with angels appearing in front of me, saving my life and then vanishing right before my eyes. God's angels always come in the form of a person or an animal to help us, then they leave. They never go bump in the night but bring peace and help in a form that you probably don't recognize as an angel. They fit in easily, and while they are helping you, many times you will move but never feel the movement. You are just suddenly transported. This was brought home to me twice that I can remember.

Once when I was swimming in the Gulf of Mexico, I had fallen asleep while floating on the water. When I woke up, the tide had carried me so far out I could barely see the shore. I wasn't used to swimming in waves, only in lakes and rivers, so didn't know about tides. I panicked.

As I started to swim, the waves kept knocking me under. Suddenly a man appeared next to me and quietly told me how to swim with the waves and I would be fine. I only took about two strokes when I was suddenly standing on the beach—no sensation of movement, I was just suddenly standing on the shore. I turned to thank him for his help, but he had vanished.

Another time I was on the 10 freeway in Los Angeles during rush hour—four lanes of solid traffic. Suddenly in front of me, there was an accident, which resulted in car after car becoming part of the pileup. Every lane was packed, and there was no way I could avoid the crash. I just cried out, "Jesus, Jesus!" Suddenly, with no feeling of movement, I was instantly in the next lane over, passing the piled-up cars. When God intervenes, you never feel any movement; you are just suddenly there.

I have many, many more experiences that are already told in my other book, *Walking the Thin Veil*. I have only included enough here to make a point.

Just remember this one thing: demons bring chaos, fear, sorrow, and loss, while God's angels bring peace, comfort, safety, and deliverance.

Most importantly, I want to point you to the One who alone can help you get your feet on solid ground and give you hope—that is my Savior, Jesus Christ. Here are some of the spiritual tools to help you navigate, especially through your senior years.

Without Jesus and the help of the Holy Spirit, I would never have survived the past twenty years. If you know Christ as your Savior, He will *never* leave you nor forsake you (Hebrews 13:5), and the Holy Spirit will guide you, if you will just ask Him (James 1:5). "If any of you lacks wisdom, let him ask of God who gives generously to all, and it will be given to you." (Proverbs 9:12) "The fear of the Lord is the beginning of wisdom." (Proverbs 9:10)

In spite of the changes that have happened in our world, I have had an incredible life. Few people get to do the things I have done—pioneering talking with animals and nonverbal people; traveling all over the United States, Canada, Europe, and many other places doing television appearances; and now, with God's help, creating a whole line of natural products that bring healing and comfort to thousands of people. In spite of all that, I have lived a life full of trials, sorrow, and loss. God never promised us it would be easy, but He did promise that He will be there to help us through the hard times.

When I first started my career with animals, God let me know in no uncertain terms, this was His will. I was deeply criticized and ostracized by a lot of Christians and churches because I talk to animals. When I was in my twenties, I was at a church service one evening when the guest preacher came down off the pulpit and got in my face, literally snarling at me. He said, "You are of Satan. What you do is evil. I denounce you. You must repent and never talk to another animal." I was devastated. I left that meeting in tears, thinking, If a man of God says that, he must be right, and I am wrong. How could I have missed God's will so badly?

I fasted and prayed for a couple of days, because if this wasn't from God, I never wanted to talk to another animal again. During my fast I started getting a lot of calls from people whose animals I had communicated with, thanking me for doing that. They recognized their animals had feelings and had been going to people in the new age and occult practices to learn what their animals felt, but because of my warnings about those practices, they had now turned back to God and their church.

At the end of those few days, God spoke clearly to me that if I would do what He called me to do and not listen to man, it would be rough, but He would justify me in time. I learned then and there to listen to counsel, but only take God's direction over theirs if their advice conflicted with God's instructions to me.

The only caution God made clear to me is that whatever I heard or learned in my work must line up with the Word of God. If it contradicted Scripture, then I was hearing the wrong voice, and I get a strong check in my Spirit. It has really been hard fulfilling the task He has called me to, but I have tried to obey Him above anyone else.

As Romans 11:29 says, "The gifts and the calling of God are without repentance." I agree. Yes, I am different, but then God uses the foolish to confound the mighty. God revealed to me that the new agers had His truths about animals long enough, and it was time to point people to the truth of how deeply the animals really feel.

He created them the way they are, and we need to respect His creation. After all, Adam and Eve had communication with the animals in the Garden of Eden; Adam even named them. Balaam's donkey talked to Balaam and asked, "Why are you beating me? Haven't I always obeyed you? Can't you 'see' the angel blocking the way?" (Numbers 22:28–31) He couldn't understand why Balaam didn't see it, because animals can easily "see" spirit beings. That donkey expressed sorrow at what his owner was doing, and Balaam even admitted to sinning because he beat the animal and disobeyed God.

You think they don't have feelings? If you really look at your pets with an open mind, you will see the intelligence and love in their eyes. They feel all the same emotions that you and I do. They are a lot smarter than we give them credit for.

One day while visiting Bryce Canyon, a national park in Utah, we observed a large raven scavenging for food. Since I was eating a sandwich, I decided to throw him a piece of bread, which he quickly ate. He stood there looking at us, so I decided to see how he would handle a whole slice of bread. I tossed it down before him and to my amazement, he circled it a couple of times, studied it, then carefully rolled it up into a roll so he could hold it in his beak and flew off with it. I could almost hear him say to his mate who was sitting on their eggs, "Hello, dear. I brought you dinner." Even a bird has incredible thinking ability. Wow! God sure made an incredible world.

I have been labeled everything from evil, to wonderful, to crazy for how I have helped people appreciate their animals better. When I was young, I was always worried about what people thought of me and didn't want to make waves, but not anymore. I know who I am in Christ; I know I have obeyed Him *most* of the time, and what other people think isn't my problem. I am only responsible to one person, my Heavenly Father through His son Jesus and by listening to and obeying the guidance of the Holy Spirit. (John 16:12) Jesus walked the earth and helped those around him, but He had to go back to the Father so He could send the Holy Spirit who indwells everyone who accepts Jesus as their Lord and Savior. He is here to guide and teach each one of us. (John 15:7–15)

I know the only way I have made it this far is because I know that God will never leave me nor forsake me. Without Him at my side, I know I would not have made it this long or survived what I have experienced. I will always be grateful to my pastors, Jack Hayford and Scott Bauer, the only two pastors who didn't ask me to leave their church when I began my work with animals. They loved me and supported me through the trials. They often told me they didn't understand what I did, but they knew my heart and felt God had His hand on my life, and who were they to question God? I was under their teaching for twenty-five years, and I am *so* grateful for their gift of love and support.

I know God has had His hand on me and protected me since I was born. Satan has been trying to kill me since I was six months old, when I came down with pneumonia in the freezing winter in New York. In those days there weren't any antibiotics, so the only treatment was to wrap me in blankets, apply a poultice to my chest, and open the windows to let the cold air shrink the alveoli in my lungs so I could breathe. All my life I have seen Satan try to kill me, and he is still at it. But God has protected me all the way.

Where did I first meet Jesus? When I was thirteen I attended a revival service in a little country church in northern New York where the preacher told me how much God loved me. "For God so loved the world (which included me) that He gave His only begotten Son (Jesus) to die for my sins so that I could have eternal life in a wonderful place called Heaven." (John 3:16 and John 5:11, 12) That day I opened my heart to Christ and asked Him to forgive my sins and come and live in my heart.

I wish I could say that from that day on I was perfect or never made bad judgments or mistakes. I can't. I know that through it all, God has forgiven me of each one and brought me to this time in my life. Many of those experiences are related in two of my books, Season's, *My Journey Through the Three Dimensions of Natural Healing* and *Walking the Thin Veil*.

It has taken most of my life to learn total obedience, but thank God He has held me through my mistakes, so that I am now in the place where I can hear the voice of the Holy Spirit more clearly. I don't do much anymore without first asking Him for direction. I sure wish I'd learned that in my early years; I would have avoided a lot of heartache.

A lot of the mistakes I made came from the fact that I was raised in a family that made those same mistakes, and as most children do, repeated them. It was our way of life, so I just fell into the same patterns.

One of the patterns I observed in my family was the way they handled their finances. If they wanted something and didn't have the money to buy it, they just went out and charged it or somehow manipulated their accounts to get it. I did the same thing for years and got into a lot of financial debt, until one day I sat down and figured out what I was throwing away each month for interest on those card balances. I was shocked, as it was money just gone that I could have used for other things. I decided there and then that I would only buy what I could pay for. I started paying off those credit cards and trusted that God would provide the item I wanted if He knew I needed it.

Things went pretty well until one day I had a chance to buy a twenty-one thousand dollar RV that I really need on the property, for the low price of three thousand, cash. Yes, it needed work, but it would have been worth it. Needless to say, I didn't have that much on hand, so I prayed about it. I knew God could provide it if He wanted to, but the old nature warred within me every day over that trailer.

God did not give me permission to go into debt to get it. I knew He was saying no, but that didn't make me want it any less. This emotional war went on until the night before they were to come and pick it up—then the old habit kicked in. It was just too good a bargain. I decided to try to manipulate the bank and go into debt to get it anyway I could.

I started to get out of my chair to go to the computer to let the bank know I was going to buy it, but as I started to get up, I felt a pressure like the heel of a hand on my chest, pushing me back into the chair. At the same time, I heard God as clear as if it had been an audible voice: "I said no!" I finally got God's message and sat back down. I even felt relief the next day as the RV was towed away. Sometimes the old nature is hard to kill, but God knows best what my future holds and why He said no. "No good thing will He withhold from them that walk uprightly." (Psalm 84:11)

The Bible calls the Holy Spirit our helper. (John 14:26 and John 16:12) This fact was never made clearer than when I was developing my product line. When I needed information, I would ask the Holy Spirit to help me get it, and sure enough, someone would call and say, "You've been on my mind. What is going on or what do you need?" And they would have the exact information I needed.

Other times I would ask God for information, only to come home to learn that someone had dropped by and left me a tape that had exactly what I needed on it. This is the reason I know my products are so effective: they were given by God.

People don't know it, but I have a learning disability. I can't retain what I memorize, especially dates and names of things. So you can understand why I relied on God to develop the products. It is His knowledge, not mine. All I did was obey Him as He told me what to do. The ability God has given me makes me able to put facts together and come up with useful conclusions.

No matter what your disability is, God will use you to fulfill the purpose for which He designed you. Sometimes I wish I had been raised differently, so I would have a sweeter, more easy-going disposition, but then again, if I had, would I have had the courage to step out and do the things I have with animals, facing such criticism? I don't think so. So just remember, He can use you for what He designed you to do, if you will just trust Him. Rejoice in that.

I love the verse that says, God uses the foolish things to confound the mighty. (1 Corinthians 1:27) Foolish because to the world, the handicapped person can't do something unusual, but in God's hands, those submitted to Him will do mighty things. Look at the young Mongoloid boy who did an incredible job of acting as an angel in the series, *Touched by an Angel*. He must have had great parents and teachers who taught him to live above his limitations.

You hear preachers on television repeatedly telling the audience to believe that God has a special purpose for your life. Just step out and believe Him, and you can accomplish great things, far above what you ever imagined. Sad to say, I think they don't really believe their own sermons, because unless you have the word *doctor* in front of your name or are somehow famous, they don't believe you or acknowledge your accomplishments. Makes me wonder sometimes just how much those preachers really believe or practice what they are preaching. God can use anyone for anything He wants as long as that person is committed to Him and will allow Him to teach them.

It is important to know who you are in Christ and experience the power available to you in the "Name of Jesus." Here are some of the miracles I and others who have seen that power in action have witnessed.

A few years ago, there was a terrible windstorm heading our way. I thought of the Scripture where Jesus tells us that we would do what He does, but even greater works will we do. Greater, I believe, because we are humans who will do them, imperfect vessels committed to Him. I thought, if Jesus can speak to the wind and the sea and immediately it was calm, couldn't He do the same through me?

I spoke to the storm in Jesus's name and told it to go around me. At that time, I just couldn't afford to pay someone to come out and clean up the debris or clear my drive since I live a quarter mile back from the road. Since all was quiet, I went on about my business and later decided to go to the store. My yard was clean, no debris, no nothing, never even heard the wind, so I just figured the storm didn't happen. As I started to drive out, I found it impassable because the roads and yards around me were covered with downed branches, so I couldn't get through! God had certainly answered my prayer.

Another time, two years ago when we had the horrible fires, I was completely surrounded by them. They were less than a mile from me and rapidly heading my way. Jane, my semi-adopted daughter that God has given me in my old age, was visiting me at the time. We were on alert to get ready to evacuate with only time to jump in the car and go. I remembered how God had saved me from the wind, so Jane and I stood on the porch and said, "Fire! In the Name of Jesus, turn around and go back up over that hill. God didn't restore my home and business to have you burn it down. You have no place here."

I live in the middle of twenty acres of very dry pastures and trees, and I knew there would be no way we could survive a fire. Everything would be gone. We watched as that fire turned around and went back up over the hill. We never had to leave. Needless to say, I have been praising God ever since.

I will share another story that happened recently. The power company knows that when a severe windstorm hits, it will blow trees over onto the power lines and sparks fly that will cause fires. In our rural area I am surrounded by dry, old forest. The utility company now turns the power off until they can check the lines and be sure they are clear. During the bad winds we had recently, we were being warned that our area was going to be shut down without further warning, and we could be out of power for days.

Since heat really makes me sick, and since it was such an unusually hot day when the storm hit, I quietly asked the Lord to keep our power on so I could keep the air conditioners going. The wind came and went, but my power never went off.

When I knew it was really a miracle of God was when my caregiver came over and showed me that every place and street around us had their power shut off, but we didn't. Now the miracle of it is this: I am on the same transformer and power line coming into our area, even being the last house on their lines. If God hadn't performed a miracle for me, when the neighbors went down there shouldn't have been power to us either, but mine didn't go off. You think you don't have a God who cares about you? I know He does, and I am *so* grateful He gave me the Holy Spirit to talk to and uphold me.

I have another friend in Georgia who told me of a miracle in her life. She said they had been having excessive rain, and things were pretty well soaked around her, even her deck. It looked like it was going to rain again so she went out on her porch and spoke to the rain clouds. In the Name of Jesus, she told them to go around her, because she needed the porch to dry out before it could be sealed by paint. Then she needed another day to paint it and at least two or three days to get the paint fully dried. She knows who her God is, and sure enough, the rain came down around her house, but her place stayed dry until the painting was done and dry.

Another time, when hurricane Ian was heading directly for their area in Florida, a group of her friends got together and prayed for the storm to bypass them. Lo and behold, the storm turned and went another direction. I also prayed for that storm to bypass my nephew's mobile home just North of Tampa, and it did.

I have another friend who also knows who her God is. When Hurricane Ian was heading toward her son's home in Florida, she started praying it would go around his house. He lives in Cape Coral, which received a direct hit with terrible force. Her son stood in his window and watched as the storm came directly at them, then suddenly stopped just before it hit them, turned, went around their property, and continued, only to get back on the same direct path it was on before it bypassed them. They experienced very little damage of any kind.

Now that I live alone and am in my golden years, I hold onto Him more than in my youth to sustain and care for me. Do I do it in every circumstance? Sorry to say, I don't. Sometimes I feel like He steps in and saves me and leaves, but I know He never does leave; we just forget He is here and taking care of things.

I was reminded of this one morning when I was worrying and fretting about the bad direction our country is taking. I was praying and praying for it to turn around, but it doesn't seem to. As I was coming out of my bedroom, I heard what was almost an audible voice say, "I've got this! Don't worry. I've got this!" Now instead of focusing on the evil in the world, I am constantly reminding myself and my clients, we need to keep our eyes on the solution, which is God, who "has it." Get our focus off the problem and back on Him with praise and thanksgiving for all He is doing to care for His children.

God dwells in the praises of His people, not in our begging. Makes for a more comfortable living if you do.

It is amazing what God will do with your life if you let Him. Sometimes His lessons are hard, but He has a purpose in how He guides us. I am one of these people who has to plan my errands ahead of time, and when they don't go off as I intended, I get frustrated and mad. God taught me one day that my plans go awry for a reason.

I don't go out much, so one Thursday when I went to the bank to do some business, I was surprised to discover they had closed early. I was terribly frustrated and mad. How could that happen to me? Now I was going to have to go out again on Saturday to do my banking and grocery shopping. I fussed over that for two days and finally dragged myself out on Saturday.

I did my banking, went to Costco, and completed my shopping. Normally, I would just go home after, but this time, for some reason I felt compelled to go to the tire store to check my tires. I don't know why I did that, as I had no reason, but I went. I sat there in my car for a while waiting to be served when a young man drove up next to me and went inside. God spoke to me very clearly that I was to pay for his tires.

When the clerk came out to look at his car, I overheard their conversation. The young man asked if they had any used tires, because he couldn't afford the new ones and his were really bad. I called the clerk over and told him I would pay for his tires. The clerk informed me the young man was going home to get the money and would be back. As they walked away, God told me the man wasn't doing that but just needed to save face, because he didn't have the money to pay for them. I just shrugged it off and a few minutes later left to go home.

I got about a mile from the store and God nearly yelled at me. If it had been an audible voice, I am sure anyone around me would have heard God shouting at me. He said, "I told you to pay for his tires; now do it." I pulled off the road and called the store. The same clerk I had spoken to at the store, answered the phone. I asked him if he had that young man's telephone number. He said he did, so I told him to call the guy and tell him to get back to the store because his tires were paid for. I went back and the bill was $150. I had exactly $155 in my wallet.

I finally felt at peace and told the clerk to tell that young man that God made me come back and pay for his tires and to thank God for them. The clerk must have been a Christian, because he let me know he would be happy to tell him.

I don't know anything about that young man and never spoke to him, but I sure hoped it had been a blessing to him. *God rearranged my whole schedule even closing the bank early so that I would be there at exactly the same time that young man was who needed help.*

God blessed me greatly by that whole incident and taught me that if the bank closes early or something happens to change my plans, that He has a reason for it, and I am to thank Him that He loves me and those around us that we can help. I learned to never question God again when things like that happen. I don't know who had the greater blessing, the young man or me.

I know God will use you, if you let him. Don't wait until He has to "shout at you." Sometimes God will speak to you to help someone else like He did the day He told me to help the young man, and other times He will show His power if you trust Him. You need to realize who you are in Christ and the power His Name carries.

I have many stories to relate of how He intervened in miraculous ways when I and a few others I have talked to have spoken in Jesus's Name to disasters heading our way. He is real and ready to help us. These stories are related in my other books.

We knew we could trust people back when I was a child, or at least mostly we could. We grew up trusting the banks and the doctors, never to question what they were telling us, because they really did care for us. Sadly, not anymore. My goal in the second part of this book is to make you aware of the things that are going on that can wreak havoc if you get caught in the many traps aimed at separating seniors from their money. Social media, TV ads, and the Internet allow thieves and scammers to do this because they don't have to face you. There seems to be very little empathy anymore and definitely no consequences for their actions.

I have related those traps from personal experience to show you how they go about snaring you. I do that so you can recognize what they are up to, should it happen to you. Hopefully it will help you avoid the pitfalls I have endured and show what resources you have available to you should you find yourself in difficulty.

Now that I have shared some of the spiritual tools available to you, let's get on to the second part of the book and the problems you may face, especially as a senior citizen.

PART TWO

CHAPTER 1

LONELINESS

This is probably the hardest thing we all face as we get up into those senior years.

I feel that I am one of the lucky ones, to have traveled all over the world, met thousands of people, and made friends that still keep in touch. Most of the time those relationships grew out of our common love for animals, especially my dog-show friends We would park our motor homes close together, and when the show was over at the end of the day, we would have a potluck dinner and play games. I used to do consultations with animals all week, sometimes flying somewhere to do a television show, but those dog shows were my social times. These friendships have helped me deal with the many losses I have experienced, and those relationships have kept me from being a lonely, childless widow now in my eighty-fourth year. I am never lonely because my animals, friends, and work fill my days.

To avoid the pitfalls of loneliness you must develop friendships and nurture them throughout your life. People just don't drop by one day and say, "Hey, I am looking to meet someone who will be my friend. Are you looking for friends?" You have to stay involved in life as much as possible. Don't think your spouse or children will meet all your needs for the rest of your life; they won't. Friends and activities you love to do are what will comfort your latter years. I like the old King James version of Proverbs 18:24 that says, "He that would have friends must prove himself friendly." This is especially true when it comes to developing those lifelong relationships. They just don't happen. You have to stay involved with others, or you will drift apart and be alone in your senior years.

I have found the best way to stay in touch is to become an encourager. Every day seek out someone who can use your help in something. It may be a helping hand, a smile, or just a compliment that will help them feel better about themselves. If nothing else, just send a text or email with an uplifting thought or joke or even a Bible verse that tells them you are thinking of them and love them. You will be surprised how that will even lift your mood too. I am a late-night person and usually go to bed about the time my neighbor is going to work, so I have tried to develop the habit of sending her an encouraging word or verse that will start her day. It is amazing how it has lifted her spirits.

The only thing that will get you through your alone years is a deep, daily relationship with our Lord and Savior, Jesus Christ. The Holy Spirit is your comforter and your guide. Knowing who you are in Christ—with the Holy Spirit to help you if you ask—gives you the resources you can rely on. Let me share a couple of things here that brought that home to me.

I own a pretty good–sized piece of property that I could take care of when I was younger, but in my latter years I can no longer keep up the mowing and raking and all else that goes with twenty acres As my strength wanes, I have also found it impossible to even clean my house properly. Every time I have needed someone, I just took it to the Lord and asked Him to send the help I needed. Over the past ten years He has done just that. When one leaves, He sends a better one. He is faithful in guiding and caring for you.

As I've started having trouble remembering where I've put things, I now just ask the Holy Spirit to show me where I left it. He knows where it is. I then go on about my business and pretty soon the thought pops into my head as to where I left it. Sure enough, when I look, there it is.

We get so busy just living—work or a career, house to run, groceries to buy, laundry piling up, run the kids to this and that event or lesson, and just busy, busy, busy. We don't stop to plan for the future—just too much to think about today. Tomorrow will take care of itself. Then it happens. One day we wake up and realize we are senior citizens, but we aren't prepared. So now what?

The children have grown up and left home, or if you are childless, you retire. That is okay because now you and the hubby can relax and travel. You finally have the time to do all the things you looked forward to all your lives—visiting friends and family you never had the time to go see, exotic places to explore, that cruise to faraway places you always wanted to take but didn't have the time or money to enjoy. Then the unthinkable happens, your spouse develops a debilitating illness or dies, and all those dreams of enjoying each other when you had time are suddenly gone.

For a while the house is still full with all your friends who came to comfort you and see how you are doing, but they gradually disappear to live their own lives, and the house becomes eerily quiet. Your children become busier and busier with the demands of their own jobs and family, and no matter how hard they try, they just have less and less time for mom or dad. Sort of reminds me of the song Harry Chapin used to sing, "The Cat's in the Cradle." If you don't know the song, look it up. It is worth the time.

Because you don't want to be a burden, you accept the loneliness. If you have not made this time as part of the "possible" plan from your youth, you are now thrown into depression and feel totally lost and alone. You have been the caregiver all your life, but now you have lost that role. Maybe your spouse is still alive but now needs constant care, but even that isn't fully satisfying. If your spouse has Alzheimer's, can you cope with the stress of endless care with no one to relieve you, so you can get away for a while or just rest? You feel like you might as well be alone when your spouse has advanced Alzheimer's, because the relationship isn't the same. (I tell you in the next chapter how to help them get well. There is a cure for Alzheimer's but your doctor won't tell you about it, because they probably don't know about it either.)

What happens now? This is when you hit the prairie dog holes I talked about in the foreword. How do lonely people cope? I will share what I have observed seniors do when this happens.

The first coping mechanism is alcohol.

I cannot tell you the dozens of women I have known as I have traveled worldwide who have turned to alcohol to drown their loneliness. Women who had had active careers suddenly find themselves alone and maybe even debilitated, or now that they are on Social Security, find they can't afford to go out anymore. You have to talk to them by ten in the morning or they are too drunk to be coherent.

They didn't intend to become alcoholics, but it started with that one lonely drink to help them relax and get to sleep at night. It helped them feel good, so when they started to feel blue, they just took an extra drink earlier in the evening. Then the feeling of loneliness hit them earlier in the day, so just one more to help them get through that heartache. On and on it goes until they are drowning in liquor.

Since they are now pretty much under the influence most of the day, they really don't go out to visit, shop, or whatever, because they can't navigate. They often get easily confused as to what they are out there for or sometimes even just get lost. It's easier to stay safely at home. Why go shopping anyway? That used to be fun and filled a gap in their lives, but at their advanced age what do they need new clothes for? They have more than they will ever wear for the rest of their lives! So why bother going out anyway? Stay home and just have another drink.

The television becomes their companion—the voice in the background to replace those who are no longer there. At least the house doesn't feel so empty. Besides, they watch show after show and live the lives of the characters in the program, getting themselves out of their own empty lives. Had they been cultivating those friendships and stayed active in clubs, etc., this probably wouldn't have happened. The loneliness wouldn't have weighed on them so heavily, and they would have stayed too busy to feel that great weight of emptiness.

The one thing I would encourage you to do is get a pet. There are thousands out there that need you just as much as you need them. If you are mobile, get a dog. It will make you get up in the morning and take them for a walk. This will keep you more mobile and get you out of that empty house. Besides, when you have a dog, people are more prone to stop and talk to you. It opens doors to getting to know people. If you are near a dog park, there are a lot of owners there who love to visit while the dogs play.

When you have a pet and have to run an errand without them, when you come home there is always someone there to greet you and make you happy you came back. You always have love and companionship. The house is never empty.

If you can't get around to care for a dog, get a cat. They can be so loving and take a lot less work. When you are sitting there or lying down, they just stick to you like glue. There is always a warm, affectionate, soft body to feel close to you, telling you how much they love you.

The second coping mechanism is the Internet.

People often wonder why so many elderly people get on the Internet and meet the Nigerian scammers. They are always twenty-one or twenty-eight years old, love older people, and always wanted to marry an older person. They talk to you, make you feel loved and wanted, filling that void that your empty house can't. Seniors hear all those wonderful words of how they are falling in love with you, can't wait to be with you, and if you will help them financially to get a visa, they will come over here and marry you. It makes no difference if you are a man or a woman, they play the game either way, and you really can't tell if it is a man or a woman on the other end of the email. They are very good at their con game and know just exactly what to say to get you hooked.

It happened to a dear friend I'd known for thirty-eight years. She was an intelligent, Bible-teaching woman and a military veteran who retired and lived in the apartment I built below my house. I never realized how lonely she felt. Her family never came to see her, and I was so occupied with my business that she spent 99 percent of her time just playing on her phone. She never let on to me that she was sending a Nigerian man money to "help his little brother get a mattress to sleep on, as he couldn't provide one," or "he had lost his job and needed to feed his kid brother, as their parents died, and he was left to care for him," or "he needed money to get his visa started so that when his brother was old enough to be left alone, he would be able to come over here and marry her." I think down in her heart she knew it wasn't real, but a fantasy of someone loving her filled a gap that was better than nothing. The only thing that stopped the money flow was her death.

I was standing in the grocery store one day talking about her with the clerks who knew her so well, when the lady behind me piped in and said the same thing happened to her grandfather. The twenty-eight-year-old girl was getting money from him to pay for her visa and passage to come and marry him. I have another friend whose aunt has been sending some guy over fifteen thousand dollars over the years and was still waiting for him to come over and marry her. It is so widespread, and the lies go on and on.

I saw a *Dr. Phil* episode that described all the ways scammers work their lies. One lady sold her home and lost everything to send a scammer two hundred thousand dollars. Her "lover" said he was stuck trying to cross the border out of the Dominican Republic and needed money to get to her. There are no borders to cross to get off the island where the Dominican Republic is located, as Dr Phil pointed out. He found the guy, who in reality lived luxuriously in North Carolina. Even with all the proof, she wouldn't give up the fantasy and wouldn't believe Dr. Phil.

They just get so emotionally caught up in the fantasy that it becomes real to them. It is like an addiction; it starts out simple but grows and grows until it is all consuming, and they can't let themselves believe it isn't true. Besides, who wants to admit they have been a fool and bit into a lie like that?

One of the ways to tell where an email is coming from is to look at the email address of the sender. If it isn't showing, go to the top of the email and hover the cursor over the sender's name and the email address will appear. If the scammer says they are from the Dominican Republic and the website address is *AF* meaning Africa (*CF* central Africa, *CA* is Canada, etc.) you know that person is lying. When that happens, shut off your computer and get out of the house where you can meet real people. The biggest red flag is when they ask you for money, so they can come to see you or for any other reason. If that happens, *run*!

Sadly, fantasy is sometimes easier to live with than the reality of loneliness and an empty future. If they do face the reality that these people are scamming them, they will feel like absolute fools. They will think to themselves, "How could I be so stupid?" They will feel that people will laugh at them if they know what they did. They just can't go back to being "alone" again. That void is so devastating and frightening, they just can't go there. It becomes an all-consuming fantasy pit. If anyone tries to make them see the reality of what they are doing, they just live in total denial. "Who are my kids to tell me, their mother or their father is being duped?" When you try to stop them, they pull back even deeper into the fantasy.

The most important thing you can do to help them is to become involved in their lives as much as possible and divert them from the scammers. Encourage them to get out to the senior dances and the activities at the senior centers. Help divert them; do not accuse them or point out their error. The more you show them these are scammers, the more they will withdraw into the fantasy.

How they get trapped in that fantasy reminds me of what I observed while in the television industry. A good actor or actress must become the person they are portraying. If the part demands one character fall deeply in love with another character, it can become so intense and real that they both begin to feel that fantasy love as the real thing. After the filming is over, the actors still feel attached to each other and often leaving their spouses, marrying their love interest from the film. Then real life hits them, and they realize the person they thought they loved turns out to be totally different from the character they played. Oops! The fantasy became a real person. These people are great actors and actresses but poor marriage material, because they can't separate reality from fantasy. I think this is why you see so many divorces among actors.

Just be aware that these pitfalls are out there and when you start to get into them, wake up and get busy with something else like your church groups, making quilts for missions, or community breakfasts. Do things to get you out of the house. Volunteer for a hotline somewhere and be there for others, encourage someone going through hard times. Bake a cake and take it to that single mother worn out from caring for her children and working long hours; encourage her. There are millions of things you can do if you just look around.

If you are still mobile, volunteer for Meals on Wheels and brighten up some lonely shut-in's day. If you aren't mobile, get some names and phone numbers from the church and call people to let them know someone is concerned as to how they are doing. Pray with them and encourage them. Get them talking about themselves and the life they have lived. You may get to hear some fascinating stories of people you didn't even know existed. You will be blessed, and you will be surprised at how much it means to someone who is alone.

Contact your senior centers and see what volunteer jobs are available. Volunteer to read to children in the local library or to sick and lonely children in the hospital who need love as they go through a major illness, or volunteer at the hospital to sit and rock newborn babies that need special cuddling. Children who don't have that will die. Maybe you could encourage or relieve a mother who is exhausted from being in the hospital with a sick child who and needs to go home to help her other children. She could use a respite that you can give her. What about the spouse dealing with an Alzheimer's patient? They may be so exhausted but can't leave their spouse alone. You could go sit with their loved one so they can get some rest and away time. You will be surprised at how good and fulfilled that will make you feel. Pray a lot over the people you help. God hears you, and it will be a comfort to them.

Whatever you do, don't sit at home alone. Someone needs you.

CHAPTER 2

DEALING WITH PHYSICAL CHALLENGES

This chapter has a lot of hard issues to deal with, but I am able to offer you some real solutions. Some of this I have in my newsletters that I put out every few months to my clients, but I willingly share them with you in the hopes that you will also benefit.

This is the time of life when we begin to lose our strength and become quite prone to dropping things. We may get a lot of bending exercise as we stoop to pick up what we've dropped, but that isn't the best way to get exercise. The first time I saw Ann Marie's drinking glass with a whole lot of rubber bands around it, I asked her why she did that. She told me it was because she had trouble holding the slick glass; so, in order not to drop it, she put rubber bands around it for a better grip. I thought she was kind of nuts until it started happening to me. She got wise quickly.

If you have problems holding your glass, there are rubber sleeves you can put on your glasses that will prevent that. They are often used around cups of hot drinks in fast food restaurants. It's a wise investment. Sadly, there isn't much more you can do about plates and paper and other things we have a tendency to drop; you just have to grit your teeth and pick it up. When I was younger, I never thought it would happen to me, but I get a lot of bending and cleaning up exercises these days. As we age, we just have to be more focused on what we are doing and make sure that anything that is breakable or spillable is handled over a table, stove, or counter. Everything seems to get heavier, and lids get tighter.

There is one thing you can do to stop you from spilling or sloshing a liquid when carrying it: put a spoon in it, and it won't slosh as you walk. It works every time, unless you get drastic in your movements or just drop it.

Balance is another *big* problem. I have found that now I am happy that my kitchen is narrow, as it keeps me close to something I can grab, should I start to fall. Falling is a real danger for us older folk, because it can result in broken hips, knees, or just plain bruising anywhere. Then there's the problem of trying to get up again. Those ads for Life Alert or Life Protect are real. I like the Life Protect device because it fits my budget much better. I don't do anything without having it on, especially now that I live alone. If I am having a diabetic episode or fall, I push the button, and they immediately notify my caregiver or call 911, if needed. Taking B6 vitamin helps to maintain balance to a degree, but even more important is *exercise* to keep your leg muscles strong. When those leg and butt muscles get weak from sitting too much, you will be far more prone to falling.

Exercise as we age just isn't as easy as it was when we were young and is much more painful. The longer we sit, the more painful it is to get up and get mobile again. It is very difficult for me to get out and walk on my uneven ground because of my handicapped knee, so I use a treadmill with handlebars that I can hold on to for support. If I use it for at least ten minutes a day, it improves my balance and helps me walk with less pain. If you live in the city, just use a walker to balance yourself and walk on the smooth sidewalks for at least ten minutes a day. You will be surprised at how much stronger you will get and how that big tummy will get smoother.

The main reason we have swollen legs and hands is due to congestion in our lymph glands. Our heart pumps the blood and keeps that circulating, but the only pump your lymph glands have, is exercise. The lymph glands are the sewer system of the body. If you don't move around a lot, the fluids back up in your system, and you get swelling all over. This is called edema.

The best low-impact exercise, if you have painful legs or back, is swimming. If you can't do that, then get some small hand-held weights and just lift them. If you can't afford the weights, then take bottles of water or canned goods and lift them up and down. They make good weights. Get one of those squishy balls to squeeze over and over to strengthen your hands. Move your feet in circles or up and down while sitting. No pain, no gain.

MOST OF ALL, YOU HAVE TO KEEP MOVING, OR YOU WILL LOSE YOUR MOBILITY ALTOGETHER

I found out that many of the twenty-four-hour fitness places will give free memberships to senior citizens. Find one near you and ask them. They have everything you need, and some even have water aerobics for seniors.

INCONTINENCE IS A BIG PROBLEM FOR WOMEN AND MEN

I was reading an article recently that said there are more sales of adult diapers for men and women than there are for baby diapers. The TV ads make you think it is embarrassing to buy them, so you need their service to have them sent discreetly. Really? That is such a normal part of life, I was never embarrassed even as a young person. Just another sales gimmick.

I will never forget the medical convention I attended a few years ago in Atlanta, Georgia. I don't remember what made the speaker bring it up, but he said he had five daughters. "I don't buy Kotex by the box, I buy it by the pallet." The room busted up in laughter because so many EMT fathers related to that situation. The best way to handle incontinence is to keep walking to keep those sphincter muscles strong, so you can tighten up when you feel yourself leaking. There are some exercises your doctor can give you that help with that too.

THERE IS A WAY TO GET RID OF ALZHEIMER'S

For those suffering from Alzheimer's, there is an answer that the government is trying to shut down but is still available to you through naturopathic physicians. It is called EDTA IV-drip chelation. One patient was observed shuffling in for treatment who was so far gone he had to be led in by the hand and could not even talk. Several treatments later, that same person talked about getting a trailer and going to visit family and travelling to all the places they missed. He was fine because EDTA chelation cleaned out the plaque in his blood vessels and his brain.

The infused solution bonds with the heavy metals and nanobacteria in your system and removes it through the urine. This is *very effective* in restoring circulation to your legs, which can be a real problem to diabetics or those who are no longer mobile. My legs and feet were black all the way up to my knees, but with chelation my circulation was restored and the black is all gone. I don't even have to wear those compression socks anymore.

Another benefit I have experienced is that now I can walk again. I had a severe knee infection, which resulted in three surgeries to clean it out. This left me crippled; I even had to learn how to walk again. For four years I never shopped at a store that didn't have an electric cart. What a delight to be able to walk all over Walmart and Costco again. I never thought it would happen in my lifetime, but chelation is working.

For those of you who don't have access to IV chelation, chelation is now available in pill form. It doesn't work as fast as the IV method, but it works. Since I could no longer afford the EDTA IV chelation I decided to try the pills. After one week of taking two each morning on an empty stomach, I had the strength to mop my floor and do some deep cleaning, something I have not been able to do in over four years. I am gaining more mental clarity and am sleeping better. I had been asking God to show me where to find the chelation pills so I could make them available to my clients. As God often does, He caused an ad to come to my business that told me where I can purchase them. Since I have been selling them, many of my clients are reporting an increase in energy along with many of the things I am experiencing.

One caution here. Since chelation leeches a lot of metal *and* minerals from your body, it is important to take extra minerals. I take the capsules in the morning and eat breakfast at least two hours later to give the capsules time to work, then in the evening I take extra minerals, some in liquid form and some in capsules. Alfalfa is one of the best sources you can use, as it pulls minerals from deep in the earth, not just on the surface.

To learn more about how and why it works, the information is in a book called, *Forty Something Forever*. Chelation only works to help rid the hard calcium plaque buildup in the brain but doesn't clear much of the soft fatty plaque or correct brain injuries.

I believe this treatment is the only possible cure for those suffering from the graphene oxide, spike proteins, and other metals that are being injected in the Covid shots. These same chemicals are now being shed on others who are experiencing strange effects like headaches, difficulty breathing, mental confusion, and terrible tiredness. I can't get close to anyone who had the shots or I suffer the above symptoms. Had I taken the shot, I am convinced I would have been dead within days, as happened to two of my little dogs when they were exposed to a vaccinated person. To learn more about how the shedding works, go to BitChute.com and look up Clif High and listen to his explanation about shedding.

Another thing that really spikes my blood sugar is when I get to close to or touch anyone who has had the so-called Covid vaccine. I discovered this when I had a friend over for dinner, sat next to her, and hugged her goodbye. Within half an hour my blood sugar shot up *over 500*. I thought that was just a coincidence or something I ate. I started checking my blood sugar every time I get near anyone who has had those shots and the same thing happens. I also get very sick for days from vaccinated people, especially when I touch them. Apparently, I am highly allergic to what they are shedding; I am just glad that I asked God if I should take the shot and He told me no. I now know why.

I have documentation from a chemist who obtained some so-called "blood clots" from an embalmer of people who had died from "blood" clots, after they got their Covid vaccine. He did extensive studies and found the clots do not have the components of blood but are strands of metals that have clumped together to form the clots that resulted in death. If you want that documentation, contact me and I will get it to you.

Since chelation bonds with and removes heavy metals from the body, it is the only answer to remove that buildup that I know of. I feel mechanics and anyone that handled a lot of chemicals in their workplace could also benefit, but there's no documentation on that yet—just my theory. You may have to do some research to find someone in your area that does chelation, but the naturopathic doctors that do the EDTA IV-drip chelation are out there. They aren't allowed to tell you much—the FDA won't let them—but it works.

HELP FOR BRAIN FOG AND SOME MEMORY LOSS

There are a couple of good nutrients on the market to help with memory. One is called Prevagen, made from jellyfish. Did you know that jellyfish don't die? They seem to live forever. When they get old, near dying age, their system reverses and they get younger. Then, when they are nearly at baby stage, their body reverses again and they grow older. That cycle just keeps going. I saw it on a Discovery Channel program where research revealed this truth. No wonder they produce something that is helpful to humans to rejuvenate the mind.

There are other nutrients out there to help with memory, but Prevagen and Focus Factor are the two I am most familiar with and the two I take. I was having terrible brain fog, walking into another room and trying to remember what I was there for. I was just forgetting things in general—more than usual. I had to write everything down or I would forget it, even the simplest things. Most of that cleared up once I started Prevagen and Focus Factor, so I'll continue to use them as long as I can.

DIABETES AND NEUROPATHY

Even though these are two possibly different problems, they are related and treated the same. A shocker I have recently learned is something that affects diabetics. Of all things, *milk* seems to raise blood sugar. When I used to eat Breyers natural ice cream made with real milk, it never seemed to bother my blood sugar, thus I never dreamed milk would affect my glucose levels.

I hadn't been drinking milk, because I found out it contains growth hormones which can cause you to put on weight. Makes sense, as milk is produced for calves to help them grow just like for children, but for adults, it causes weight gain. Well, since it had never seemed to bother me before, I decided to have a glass of milk with my dinner. What a shock, as my blood sugar shot up to nearly 300 within a few minutes. I have a lot of problems with my blood sugar dropping dangerously low around 5 p.m., so the next time it did, I drank a glass of milk instead of sugary candy or soda, and sure enough, it brought my blood sugar back up to a safe level. Who would ever expect that skim milk would do that?

The other thing I found that raises blood sugar levels is sugar-free candy! I have tested my glucose levels after eating them and found it raised my levels no matter how little or how much I ate of it. I am not sure why, but it does. Check it out for yourself.

If you are a diabetic, I highly recommend testing your blood sugar (glucose) levels often to find out what foods affect you. If you are testing the old way by pricking your fingers and you are on Medicare, contact one of those companies that make the monitor that sticks to your arm. *Those devices are wonderful* and enable me to test my sugar levels often, *with no pain*! Your doctor can get you a prescription to help you get it at a much lower cost. Well worth the investment and *so* easy to use.

One of the biggest problems diabetes causes is damage to the kidneys, so it is important to protect them. My Kidney and Bladder formula along with extra cranberry concentrate and D-Mannos (especially good for dogs with kidney problems) helps to support and rebuild the kidneys. I learned about the cranberry juice from a friend who had kidney failure due to never drinking anything but Cokes and sodas all day. Her kidney doctor told her she now had to drink only water and cranberry juice, which she did, and her kidneys rejuvenated.

Those carbonated drinks don't just kill the kidneys, they also cause osteoporosis. Even the diet ones will cause your bones to become brittle, plus they also cause you to gain a lot of weight. You wouldn't think that of diet soda, but the only thing good about diet soda is the word *diet*. The sweetener aspartame is basically wood alcohol, the stuff that is in moonshine. That's one of the reasons diet sodas are so addictive.

Diabetics often suffer from neuropathy and foot and leg pain. I don't know of anything that will totally correct that, but the herb berberine has helped me quite a bit. With problems like that we are prone to sit even more, which is the worst thing we can do. Dry skin is behind a lot of the feeling of "pulling" on the skin, so keep your skin lubricated with good quality lotions and deep, deep massaging of the feet.

Poor circulation is the biggest culprit behind the numbness. You have to keep moving. If you can't walk often then when sitting, keep your feet moving by twisting them in circles and using devices that stimulate leg muscles like the Revitive machine. If you sit with your feet up for an extended period of time such as in a recliner and they go numb, just stand up or at least lower your feet, and it should take a lot of the numbness away. Sometimes elevating your feet helps circulation, but too long can also cause trouble.

Two more things. You have to keep your feet and legs warm to aid the circulation. One of the best ways to do that is with what is called an electric lap blanket. It is small enough to cover you up to your knees, but be sure you have cloth of some kind between it and your skin. I have always had cold feet but overall am too hot to be covered by a full heated blanket when I go to bed. I find the lap blanket over a sheet or light blanket warms my legs beautifully. You can get them for as low as twenty-five dollars. Makes all the difference for comfort. My nephew has trouble getting to sleep when he gets into a cold bed. His wife got him one of those blankets, and now the bed is warm when he gets in. He goes right to sleep.

Be careful of the shoes you wear. The more closed in and tighter the shoe, the worse the neuropathy will get. I find that open-toed sandals really make a big difference, as long as you have good arch support.

Diabetics have a tendency to get dehydrated. That makes you sicker than anything else you will experience as well as drying out your skin even more. The young people who carry a bottle of water with them have it right, as it is important to sip water throughout the day. Your body can only absorb four ounces every half hour so if you gulp down a glass of water you will only be flushing your kidneys instead of hydrating your body.

Finally, the *best* food for lowering blood sugar is *cabbage,* as well as most green vegetables, but cabbage tops the list. Supplements that work well are Ceylon cinnamon—and if you can't get that, then just plain cinnamon—and berberine.

There is one, and only one, *cure* for Diabetes that I *know* of. It happens when you get stomach bypass surgery.

There is something near the pancreas that is clipped off during the surgery, and diabetes is instantly cured. This surgery to clip that item is commonly performed in Europe but is only allowed here in the United States when you have a stomach bypass surgery.

My nephew was born a juvenile diabetic and suffered with weight control all his life. He had the stomach reduction surgery in his forties, and after the surgery he *no longer has diabetes*. It's sad that our medical profession won't do it without the weight loss surgery. I guess Big Pharma won't allow it, because diabetes brings them too much profit in all the insulin, drugs, and diabetic paraphernalia. They aren't about to let that fat cat out of the bag.

RESPECT

One of the things that irks me most is the way doctors and other professionals talk down to seniors. They think that just because we are old we suddenly became stupid. Not everybody who makes it to their senior years gets Alzheimer's or dementia.

It reminds me of a story I once heard about an older man who just wanted to get out with people, so he became a greeter at Walmart. He was often late for work so the manager called him in one day and chewed him out, like he would treat a young kid. "What happened to you as a young man when you were late?" Didn't they fire you?" to which he replied, "No, sir. I was saluted and asked 'Major, sir, could I get you a cup of coffee, sir?'"

One doctor in the ER said to me, "Now dear, don't take anything on your own, but let us prescribe the antibiotic. Leave that up to us professionals." I wanted to let him have it because of his demeanor. I have completed the pre-med program, was a trained medic, and studied a great deal of continuing medical education. I traveled extensively with Dr. Cain, a genius doctor who flew all over the world treating difficult cases no one else could help. I will always be grateful to him, as he freely shared his knowledge with me.

On Social Security, some doctors can be out of my financial reach, so since I have the medical knowledge, I often take care of myself. If I had had the money to go to medical school, I would have been a doctor; I am not stupid about medical things. I just can't prescribe certain medicines, so I have to go to a physician to get them. That was the only reason I was there, but that doctor talked to me like I was a blithering idiot.

In talking with many of my senior friends, it seems doctors have a tendency to treat seniors as though they are ignorant. This has been a common experience nearly every time I consult with professionals in many fields, not just medicine. The lack of respect for who that older person may have been in their career is appalling. How do they know that the senior citizen they are dealing with hadn't been a doctor or a pharmacist? My only comfort is knowing that the "idiot" treating me will be old someday too, and he will know how it feels.

ARTHRITIS

No matter what pains you have in your joints, the doctors automatically call it arthritis. When I went through that knee infection, I tried to tell the doctor it was not arthritis, as that comes on slowly, and what I had just suddenly happened. They just gave me a little smile and sent me home with a bottle of ibuprofen. Three weeks later I ended up in the ER where that doctor also called it arthritis, even though by now my knee was the size of a basketball. I refused to leave the ER until they aspirated to see what was really going on. They found that I was so full of infection, I was about two days away from dying of sepsis. It had gotten so bad, it required three surgeries to clean it out. If I had followed their inaccurate diagnosis, I would have died four years ago.

What shocked me even more was when my nephew in Florida ended up at his doctor's office with knee pain and was told the same thing: "Oh, it's just arthritis. You're getting up to that age now, you know." Thankfully, he went to another doctor and demanded more testing only to find out that he too had a knee infection. It had gone from his knee down to his ankle and put him out of work for weeks.

Doctors automatically assume every pain you have as a senior citizen is arthritis. Don't let them get away with that, but demand more diagnostics. If your doctor won't check further, find another doctor. There are plenty of them out there ready to treat you.

Dr. Harry Diehl, a chemist at the Laboratory of Chemistry of the National Institute of Arthritis, Metabolic, and Digestive Diseases in Bethesda, Maryland, was commissioned by the government to find a cure for the arthritic calcium build up in the joints, often due to injuries earlier in life. He did, and it is FDA approved. It is called cetyl myristoleate. The AMA kept it under patent for fifty years and wouldn't even give it to the doctors to prescribe or even let them know about It. Too much money for the pharmaceutical companies to gain in all those pain killers and joint replacements. The patent is off, so now it is available to anyone, under several trade names. Ours is called Artho-Flex.

Doctors get kickbacks from all those prescriptions they write, so be careful. As soon as you reach sixty, they start shoving pills at you. "Oh, you don't have a problem yet, but if you take these pills, it will prevent them." I experienced this when I had to spend the night in the hospital on a heart monitor.

Just before bedtime the nurse came in with a container of pills. I asked her what she was doing. She informed me that my doctor had prescribed them. I was shocked, as he knew I didn't take drugs, and yet tried to push them on me. I asked her to explain what they were for. Well, one was for high blood pressure, which I didn't have; one was for my liver, which I can eat iron for, and it doesn't bother me; another was for the side effects I would have from the liver pill; and an aspirin as a blood thinner, which I didn't need, because I didn't have a blood problem. I refused all that stuff and told her to take them back and give them to the doctor; he needed them more than I did.

Once they get you hooked, you can hardly get off of them. When we were young, we thought of doctors as minor deities and never questioned what they told us to do. Doctors who treat seniors just assume because you are old, you will have all those problems. They expect you will be compliant when they prescribe all those drugs, so they can get you hooked and make more money off their prescriptions.

I talked to my friend Sharon, whose bowel had shut down. I found out the medicine she was taking closed down the action of the intestines, so that no matter what she did, she couldn't produce a bowel movement. That particular drug also slowed the heart, and it turned out that she already had a slow heartbeat and a pacemaker. She got off the drug and, slowly, with natural herbs in my liver formula and extra magnesium, her intestines started working again, and she gradually regained her normal body functions.

Another lady in Ohio was having all kinds of problems, emotional and physical. She couldn't figure out why until she started reading me all the medications the doctors were prescribing. I couldn't believe she took so much. After we waded through the lists and looked at all the side effects, she realized that most of the symptoms she was experiencing were a result of the drugs. Had she continued on with all she was taking, she would not have been alive for probably even another year. After she got down to what she actually needed, she has been doing pretty well.

I see and hear of this all too often, and instead of cutting down the medication, they just give you more to offset the side effects of the original drug. Look them up on the Internet or go to the library and look up the drugs. Your pharmacist is also a very good source, as they know the side effects of all those drugs.

I went through a time recently when I was feeling dizzy and off balance a lot. I was also starting to experience a slight rise in my blood pressure, so I asked my doctor what I could use. He knew I was also having dizziness problems but just prescribed a drug to lower the blood pressure, because he thought the elevation was what was causing the dizziness. I asked the pharmacist if there any side effects to the drug, and he told me, yes, it causes dizziness. Wow. And I wanted that drug when I was already having problems? I don't think so.

As we age, our blood pressure normally runs in the 130s; not a big deal. It is the lower measure, the diastolic, that is important to watch. If it gets over 100, you are in danger of a stroke. Lycopene, which is derived from tomatoes, is a natural nutrient that helps lower blood pressure.

KNOW WHAT DRUGS YOU ARE TAKING
LOOK THEM UP ON THE INTERNET AND YOU WILL SEE ALL THE SIDE EFFECTS
QUESTION THE DOCTOR AS TO WHY YOU ARE TAKING THEM

Doctors don't like you to question them, but it is your body, and you have a right to know what you are putting into it. It's a good thing my friend Ann Marie questioned her doctor about a drug he wanted her to take. Her doctor already knew she was allergic to that particular drug but was trying to get her to take it in a generic brand. She had researched it and refused it. The doctor was so mad, he asked her who she thought she was to question him!

When you listen to the drug commercials on TV and hear all the side effects, who would want to take that chance? In one ad for the once-every-six-months shot to prevent bone loss, it says that it is a *rare* side effect that may cause you jawbone problems. What they are talking about is that it can cause your jawbone to deteriorate. Rare until it happens to you, like it did to one of my clients. She called me crying because her jawbone was disintegrating right after she had the shot, and they couldn't stop it. She wanted to know if I had any product or suggestion to help her. Unfortunately for her, I didn't.

I also talked to a friend of mine who said it happened to her neighbor who had been taking those shots. Her jaw disintegrated so badly she lost all of her teeth. She finally stopped the shots and started on proper nutritional supplements. Some of her jaw was restored enough to enable her to get implants at four thousand dollars a tooth. All because she believed the ads and the doctors. It wasn't so rare for those people.

Your body needs to shed old bone and rebuild it with new protein and minerals, not just calcium. Those shots stop that process. A good nutrient to take to clear up bone loss or prevent it is vitamin K2. It helps the body lay down new bone. That is not like the regular vitamin K that causes clotting, but K2, that targets bone building. It helps prevent osteoporosis too, which is one of the side effects of drinking too much soda pop, as all soda leeches calcium from the bones.

MDs are not trained in nutrition except for one organic chemistry class that tells how molecules work in the body. They learn nothing more unless they study on their own. All they are *allowed* by the AMA to prescribe is pills and more pills to offset the side effects of the first pills they prescribed. If they recommend natural vitamins or herbs, they will have their licenses to practice revoked, and they have no recourse to get it back. They are not allowed to recommend any nutritional products, except for what the pharmaceutical companies make.

We saw that not long ago with a doctor near us in southern Washington. He prescribed vitamin C and other more natural nutrients. One day, with his patients present, police-like officers wearing face masks and threatening everyone with guns, invaded his office and confiscated all his records. They closed his practice. I have heard of another doctor in Texas who had recommended vitamin C also had his office raided the same way by the gestapo and was shut down.

After twelve years of study and thousands of dollars to get to where they are now practicing, most doctors will not take the chance to dare to recommend anything natural. If you are having success with nutrition or herbs, the most they will say is, "I don't know what you are doing, but it is working, so keep it up." I feel so sorry for doctors who really care about their patients and are not allowed to do anything but shove pills down them.

Be your own advocate, and don't just jump at whatever they tell you! Question everything! If they give you too much trouble and refuse to answer, find another doctor.

Some doctors in recent years look at older people as dispensable. My friend has an eighty-nine-year-old husband who was having difficulty swallowing. She took him to the doctor and asked to have a scope done to see if he was developing cancer or ulcers. The doctor refused, as he claimed her husband was too old to do a scope. "Besides, if he has cancer at his age, we wouldn't treat it anyway. Just put him on hospice."

She was furious and went over his head and made so much fuss, they finally got another doctor who was willing to help. Thankfully, they found it was only a vitamin pill that had stuck in his throat, which eventually melted and went down, but to get him treatment, she became a tiger of an advocate for her loved one. If you get a doctor who treats your loved one like that, fight for your family. If you don't, no one else will.

Overmedication is what killed my father. At the time he was having three different problems, so was seeing three different doctors. Each doctor kept their patient records on paper, not on computers like they do now. This prevented any doctor from knowing what any other doctor was giving the patient unless they asked. None of them asked. Unbeknownst to one another, they were prescribing medicines that were reacting to what the other doctor was giving. That resulted in dad dying from leukemia due to the conflicting drugs, not of any of the physical problems he was having. Thankfully, with the invention of the computer, your medical records are available to all your doctors, so that doesn't usually happen. Sadly, once a wrong comment or diagnosis is put on your record, you can't get it removed, so be vigilant.

Usually, if you are taking more than three different medications per day, they will react against each other, causing more damage than the original problem. This really came home to me when I took my friend to the ER one night. When the doctor came in, I watched him go over chart. I was in shock. Morphine, Percocet, Valium, and a whole lot more mind-altering drugs, all in one day! I asked the doctor if he was trying to kill him with all those heavy drugs. No wonder I'd had the feeling he had become drug addicted: here was the doctor prescribing more narcotics for his old back injury. He said he had to prescribe more and more because my friend had built up a tolerance to all that he was on, so needed more and more to do the job.

My poor friend, an intelligent man who had gone through medical school but dropped out just before becoming an intern. He never wanted to be a doctor but did it only to please his dad. He then went to work as a mail carrier, which was what he had always wanted to be anyway. No wonder this brilliant man could no longer think straight and properly handle his affairs.

His wife, Mary, also a very intelligent career woman who designed fashion shows and their costumes, is also on so many drugs that she too is getting dementia. It breaks my heart to see them push those pills on them. Thank God the law is making facilities back off on some of these drugs and stop the gushing flow of opiates, but, unfortunately, for many it is too late. Addiction isn't just the drug user on the street, but older people that the medical profession shoves pills at to shut them up while making a profit on the prescriptions.

You have to be your own advocate and stand up to them. One time when I was young, I was told I was suffering from carpal tunnel syndrome. I had never heard of that before, so I contacted another neurologist to get a second opinion and test. I knew what that test involved, just hooking up some electrodes to see the nerve patterns in my arms. I also knew what it cost.

Before he started, I informed the doctor that I just wanted a second opinion but had my own doctor to do the surgery. Would he be willing to do the test? He said yes, so I had it done. Yes, indeed it was carpal tunnel syndrome, he said, so I should proceed with the surgery.

When I went to pay the bill, he had added hundreds to the bill, probably more than what the surgery would cost. I was never warned about this, and all he could say was, "After all, you aren't coming back here to have me do the surgery, so why not pay me more?" I was pretty angry and probably shouldn't have replied like I did, but I wrote him a check for the amount of what the test actually cost. I informed him I wasn't buying him his new Mercedes or paying for his son's college tuition. I was just a simple working stiff willing to pay fair-market value. He never sent me a bill.

You have to stand up to them. You don't need to get nasty, just firm, or they will shove needless pills at you and keep you running back again and again. After all, old people are sick, aren't they? They just assume you are and that you will do what they tell you to.

Please be careful. Many older people are lonely and addicted to going to the doctor for every little thing. We grew up in the generation that didn't question what the doctor told us to do, after all they were educated and you older people aren't, so who are you to question them? We were taught to pay the bill, shut our mouth, and, most of all, don't ask questions. I think the younger generation is not so *gullible*.

LIVER PROBLEMS

Depression can have a physical cause. When you have blood work done, the results will show that your liver is working; they just don't say if it is congested or not. Sometimes the test won't even reveal if it is working well or not. When you are on medications, many of them damage the liver, which can result in manic depression. I had a client in California who was experiencing such a condition, and no one could figure out why. All the doctors did was give her more and more antidepressants. All she would do was sit in a chair by the window and stare all day. She did nothing and rarely talked.

When I met her, I recognized what was going on, so I suggested her caretakers think about taking her off all those meds that were making her into a zombie, and I recommended my liver capsules of natural herbs to clean out and rebuild her liver. They followed my advice, and in less than a week she was back to normal and planning a cruise with friends. She became quite the chatterbox.

Another side effect of a congested or damaged liver is the appearance of brown spots on your hands, arms, and face. These are called liver spots for a reason; they are a result of liver problems. The best way to clear them up is by cleaning up and rebuilding your liver. Our liver formula does that beautifully, and when they start to appear on me, I just increase the number of capsules I am taking, and they fade away. There are herbs out there that most people know of, like milk thistle, to clean the liver, but you also have to rebuild it so it can function effectively.

One of the strangest phenomena I have learned about the liver is, if it can't handle or process something, that is the very thing you will crave. I don't understand it, but it is true. One of the things that affects the liver is sugar. Your liver has a hard time processing it, but, weirdly, it makes you crave it. If you are a sugar-holic, you are in danger of becoming an alcoholic, or if you are an alcoholic trying to get off liquor, you might crave sugar. That is because sugar and alcohol break down into the same molecules once they are processed through the liver.

Did you know that the liver is the only organ in the body that will regrow if you lose part of it? I believe that is because everything you eat has to be converted into living body cells by the liver and all waste in the blood has to be eliminated through the blood cleansing done by the liver. God knows how important a good working liver is, so I believe He designed us to be able to regrow whatever we lose or damage to keep us alive and functioning well. Not just alcoholics develop cirrhosis of the liver; other things can cause it too.

HAIR LOSS AND HAIR THINNING

Hair loss is usually connected to a weakened immune system, and when it is severe it is called alopecia. It is an autoimmune problem that causes you to lose *all* the hair on your body, not just on the head. The only thing I can suggest here is to try to fix your immune system and add collagen to your diet, because collagen can help hair grow and thicken. I have never been able to get my hair to grow past my neck; it always broke off and is so thin. (Inherited that from my mother.) I always wore wigs for my public appearances, because my own hair is such a problem. I added collagen to my diet about two years ago, and my hair is now halfway down my back. Sadly, it still didn't thicken, but it seems to for some people. Collagen is the number one protein needed to strengthen and repair your tendons, skin, and nails. This is a great antiaging nutrient for your overall looks.

For those of you who have small dogs that have collapsed tracheas, I recommend adding collagen to their diets too. It is where the cartilage in the throat softens and collapses, causing them to cough. Food often gets in the folds of the throat and causes infections. After you kill the infection and use the proper cough syrup, I highly recommend adding collagen to their diet to help rebuild and strengthen the cartilage, to keep the throat open. I did this with one of my Chihuahuas, and he rarely coughs anymore.

SKIN PROBLEMS

You may also want to add some Hyaluronic acid to your diet. It is the nutrient that makes the cells of your body retain fluids and lubricates your joints. As we age, our bodies don't produce enough of it, and our skin begins to sag, bruise easily, and gets so wrinkled it looks like it needs to be ironed. Sadly, if you are a smoker, no amount of nutrients or lotions will be able to do anything about the terrible wrinkles you will develop.

The other problem the deficiency creates is in your eyeballs. They begin to shrink, causing light to flash out of the corner of your eyes. Hyaluronic acid will fill the eyeball back out, and the flashes will stop. Combining the collagen with the Hyaluronic acid, you will have younger looking, healthier skin too.

The final thing I want to talk about is not a pleasant subject, that we older folk don't like to do, and that is proper bathing. When I went into homes as an EMT, you could always tell it was an older person's home—you could smell it. The more medications you take and the less you eat a balanced diet of fresh fruits and vegetables, you will have problems with body odor. It is hard to fix healthy meals because who wants to cook for one person? But if you want to stay healthy and mobile, you just have to make yourself do it. Sometimes I will cook up a big meal, which looks like I am having a lot of company; I then divide it up into normal portions and freeze them to use when I don't feel like cooking, which is most of the time these days. It is convenient, easy, and balanced.

I believe the reason seniors don't bathe more is linked to the fact that it gets harder and harder to get out of the tub. I can get in but wouldn't be able to get out, so I stick strictly to using the shower. If you can afford it, the most ideal tub is a walk-in tub. They are wonderful. I tried one at my friend's house and loved it. Unfortunately, the companies won't install one in a mobile home, which is what I live in.

Many older people will even avoid taking showers, because they are afraid of slipping, so here are some safety tips. Add a shower chair to sit on while you bathe. You can also add inexpensive bars to hold on to that are anchored to the wall by suction cups. To prevent slipping, you can get plastic drawer or sink liners or rubber mats to put on the floor of the shower, but cut a hole in the middle of it so the shower can drain. Use a nonskid bath mat to be sure you don't step onto anything slippery. I keep the shower chair right by the shower so I can safely sit to dry myself off.

It is recommended to only shower a couple times a week, so your skin doesn't dry out too much, and in between showers, I always take a couple of minutes to sponge bathe the odiferous parts. Powder helps a lot, and a little cologne helps prevent odor, and you or your house will never have that *old person* smell. If you live in a hot climate where you perspire a lot, you will need at least a simple rinse off more often, with minimal soap.

Since so many of us "leak" as we age, it is very important to stay clean, especially for diabetics who have a stronger urine odor. There is an excellent soap called Mother Dirt, a probiotic skin, face, body and hair care soap that puts good, healthy, odor-eating bacteria back on to your skin, bacteria that is lost during bathing with regular soaps. The link to it is https://motherdirt.com.

If you are having problems caring for yourself but don't need constant care, contact your local senior center or your state officials that care for seniors, and ask for help. There are a lot of resources out there that will get you part-time care. Don't be too proud to ask for help; they are being paid to be there for people like you and really do want to help. *Pride is a poor bedfellow.*

Having trouble falling asleep at night? Here is one suggestion I found that works for me. Your brain is active all day and sometimes just won't shut off so you can sleep. I find that having a routine before bed gets your mind thinking, "Oh, it is time to shut down." Feeding my animals is the final chore of the day. Then I prepare for bed, and the last thing I do is sit on the side of the bed and do easy, large-print crossword puzzles. I will usually sip something that relaxes me like a hot chocolate or a glass of wine, and by the time I have finished my drink and the puzzle, my mind is shut down and I go right to sleep. Try something that is very relaxing to you, but make it a routine, and it should help.

CHAPTER 3

RECOGNIZING SCAMS

The stores have a new wrinkle in marketing: they offer *big* discounts on items they know their patrons will go for, but in order to get that big discount, you have to download the store's app. This gives you access to the digital coupon needed to take advantage of the savings. They aren't giving you the bargain to draw you into the store so you will buy more; the real purpose is to make money on your information.

The minute you download that app, the store has access to your phone. They can download all your contacts and everything you are interested in looking at to possibly buy. This is done so they can use your preferences to target their ads to you and so they can sell your information to other marketers. That is how they get their money back for the low price on the discounted item.

On many of their apps, unbeknownst to you, you are giving them permission to download everything on your phone, including your photos, etc. Sometimes you have to give them permission to access your phone, but in many of them it is either implied or you don't see the fine print that gives them that access.

If you find that digital coupons save you a great deal of money, then get a cheap burner phone that you use only for downloading apps and digital coupons, thus protecting what you have on your private phone.

The burner phone is particularly important for those who take nude selfies and send those photos to friends or lovers. That prevents those downloading your information from accessing your personal phone to look at and sell those photos to unscrupulous people. These people are very clever, and even though the company app is legitimate, the people processing your information may be looking for things they can take off your phone to sell. Pornography is a hot money-making item.

I was watching the *Dr. Phil* show one day, when they were talking with individuals who were asking how their nude photos got hacked. I believe this is one way, so be wise and get a burner phone, so they have no access to your private information. Better yet, don't take naked selfies, and you won't have those creeps knocking at your door or exposing you to your boss, which could cost you your job. Exercise some self-respect and keep that part of your life private.

Another one of the latest scams is the Publishers Clearing House. These scammers are trying to get your personal and bank information. They tell you that you are Publishers Clearing House's grand-prize winner of millions of dollars. Then they tell you you have to give them your bank information, so they can transfer the money, but instead of transferring money into your account, it will be transferred out.

The other approach is, if you are over sixty-five, they will also give you an additional amount and a new Mercedes car. Everyone knows about the big giveaway with that company, and they appeal to your strong desire to win it.

The first person that called me using that scam wanted my information and further stated that they needed me to give them $500 to file with the state of New York to be able to transfer the millions. That caller had a Seattle phone number, and it was about a year ago. Recently, I received a new call from New York where they told me I was the grand-prize winner, but I'd never even entered. They used the same tactics they had used a year earlier. It didn't work the first time, and I wasn't about to bite into that scam the second time either.

I used to enter those contests, and one time I called Publishers Clearing house to see who won only to be told that no one drew the winning number. They are appealing to your natural desire to get rich quick. They are counting on you buying from their catalog, because many people think they have a better chance of winning if they do. Before I became a senior citizen, I was on a dog-show trip to Alaska. My senior friend who was with us kept telling me to hurry and get home before the date the contest winner was announced. She seriously thought they would come to her home and tell her she had won the millions.

Don't buy into it, and never, ever give your personal or bank information to anyone over the phone. Always call the bank, utility, or company they claim to represent to be sure the call is legitimate. The biggest red flag is when they tell you that you have to buy right away or the sale will be off. Not true; it is just to emotionally rush you into getting the item.

Sometimes the scammers lose track of who they called and will try again later. That happened one day when I got a call from someone who said he was from our electric company, and because my bill was late, they were sending someone out to remove my meter. I could stop the process if I went to the store, bought a preloaded credit card, and got it to them immediately.

I went to the store and while I was looking at the cards, someone came up to me and asked if I was getting one to pay an electric bill. I was shocked she would know what I was doing. She informed me that it was a scam, as the electric company would never deal with their customers that way. I called the electric company, and they informed me it was a scam. They would never do that. I almost bit and paid the crook. I am so thankful God sent that person to stop me. I don't know if she was a real angel who took on a human form to help me or not, but to me that day, she was an angel.

When your emotions are involved, especially at our advanced age, it is hard to think quickly. I even went to the extent of having friends sit by the meter with guns so they couldn't take the meter and shut off the power—that is how convincing that scam artist was. The scammer even had my private cell phone number. Because he initiated the call to my private phone, it was even more convincing. But thinking about it, I realized the phone company didn't have my cell phone number, only my land-line number. When he called me back to see if I had gotten the card, I let him know I was aware he was a scammer and hung up on him. A year later he tried the same scam again, to which I replied, "It didn't work a year ago; what makes you think it will work now"? He hung up.

I have a wonderful friend who really has fun with those crooks. When one called her saying he was from the IRS; she pretended she was shocked. She kept saying, "Oh no, what do I do? Where do I send the payment?" She kept him on the phone, and when she got tired of it, she stopped and told him she knew it was a scam and was turning his number over to the FCC. He hung up.

The biggest scams seem to be online ads for those great miracle supplements that will "cure" diabetes and other major diseases. They start out making you listen to their spiel for twenty minutes, promising to tell you what the great food or nutrient is that will cure you. Finally, if you listen long enough, they will tell you they will sell you that nutrient for X amount of dollars and if you order today, you will get an even bigger discount. I have bitten into those three times, and all three times the product didn't work. Usually there is a hidden membership they automatically sign you up for. Then if you don't get hold of the company right away, they will keep renewing the membership and keep tapping your bank account forever.

You have to be *so* careful to whom you donate or order from over the phone or online. Most of the time you think you are ordering one item or donating to a worthy cause as a one-time gift, only to find out the item you purchased signed you up for monthly donations or memberships to their newsletter or services.

My son-in-law lost $450 in one month that way, because he had no idea that what he ordered was going to be taken out every month. He signed up for a "talk to the doctor" when you need to and was led to believe that the fee he paid was for a one-year membership in which the calls to the doctors were otherwise free. It turned out to be a monthly fee, and the calls to the doctors would then be an additional $50 charge. He is in a long-term care facility and definitely didn't need another doctor's opinion or a monthly membership. I got it stopped, but because he didn't cancel the membership withing thirty days, they took another $46, which he couldn't get back.

You have to be *so* careful. Ask anyone you deal with on the phone or Internet, before you give them your card number, if there is a membership attached to the purchase. Are they going to take out more money if something isn't stopped within a certain time? Is this fee a charge to try their product or part of the purchase, and if not cancelled, will you be charged more? Be sure you are dealing with legitimate companies, not some new person you've never heard of before. Call the company they claim to represent to be sure that is really their ad and get the exact terms before you make the purchase or agreement.

Once you get hooked, the only way you can stop these people is to have your credit or debit card changed so they can't get into your accounts, otherwise many of them will keep sucking money out each month. Be careful. Find out the details of what you think you are buying, and if it seems like a great deal, it probably isn't. Great deals usually turn out to be bad deals. You get something for free as a trial, then they hit you. And since the bank says you gave them the card, it implies they are free to use it again. You are stuck with other charges until you change that card.

I watch my daughter's and son-in-law's accounts for them, and one day I saw a charge of $59.95 on their account for *Meaningful Beauty*. I asked them if they had purchased it, and they said yes. The ad on the TV said it was on sale for $49.95. After what I had been through with the other scam that had hit me, I decided to call and check on what was really going on.

I was informed that the company had signed my daughter up for a yearly membership where she would be paying $59.95 every month for the rest of her life. What she signed up for was the original product, which cost $178. It was not $49.95 like the TV promo said, but payable monthly for $59.95, and every three months they would send her another package of product. The ad appears to be a one-time purchase for $49.95; there was nothing about it being a down payment on the $178. My daughter is in a long-term care facility because she has MS and can't function on her own and has no short- or long-term memory. When I asked her what she had done, she didn't even remember ordering anything, much less a lifelong membership for cosmetics. She wouldn't be able to figure out how to use it anyway. They knew she had limited mental ability and took advantage by selling her something when she had no idea what she was doing.

I make sure my daughter and son-in-law have what they need, so two weeks later when we finally received the package, I returned it immediately. I always pay for the return, so I have a tracking number to be sure I know when they receive it back in their facility. Fifteen days later, after I knew they already had the original package back, unopened, they charged a second payment. It took me a month of calling and calling to get their money back. Each agent I contacted told me they put in a request for the refund, but it wasn't until I threatened to contact the Better Business Bureau or take action, that they finally refunded the full price.

If you are interested in what they are selling, be sure you ask a lot of questions as to how much they are taking and when. Be sure you don't get hooked into buying a membership. I have talked to several of my friends about this after catching what happened to my daughter and son-in-law. One told me the same thing happened to her ninety-year-old mother who was caught in the same trap and lost thousands. It is a mess getting it cleared up, so always ask lots of questions. If they don't want to answer them, hang up. There is a catch somewhere.

It is so sad that everywhere we seem to go, someone is trying to get our money in a deceitful way, especially tricking the elderly. My brother and I were the two in our family who helped our parents when they were having financial difficulty. Their air conditioner died, so they contacted a salesperson from the air conditioner store. In Florida, the elderly suffer from the heat, so we knew it was necessary for them to get it replaced. We thought everything was fine until my dad died and my mom went into a nursing home. That is when we found out the truth.

They lived in a little two-bedroom, seven-hundred-square-foot home in Sarasota, Florida. The salesperson had sold them a central air-conditioning system that cost thousands, strong enough to cool an office building. That salesman took advantage of two elderly, sick people, telling them they had to have that particular central-air unit, as anything smaller wouldn't handle their needs. That house was so small and compact, a window air conditioner could have kept it cool.

My brother, a very good, strong businessman, reached the company and informed them that he knew they had cheated our parents and that he would only pay off the unit at half the price. If they refused, he was prepared to take them to court. They settled.

Because my products are known all over the world, most of my orders are shipped via the post office. That leads me to the situation I encountered. If you own a business and do a lot of shipping using online shipping companies, you really need to be aware of what is going on. They could be stealing thousands from you, and you wouldn't even know it. This is how I caught them.

I had been printing my labels online for years, so the post office could pick up the packages here at my home, a convenience this eighty-four-year-old, handicapped woman deeply needed. This turned out to save me about 5 percent than shipping at the post office, not fifty percent like the guy on TV says he saved by using this online shipping service. It was an outright lie. The online shipping companies are huge, so you wouldn't expect them to be dishonest, right? Again, my trusting nature came to the front, and I signed up.

The way it works is like this: The shipping label company has access to your bank account to draw out money, so you have funds in that company's "bank" to draw from to pay for shipping the packages. I would normally put in a hundred dollars on average, which made it possible to send out quite a few packages. It sure seemed like I was using up that reserve awfully fast, but I didn't think to sit down and check to see where the money went. They are a big company, right? They wouldn't cheat a small company like me, would they?

This went on for years, until one day I sat down and looked over the history of my shipping and noticed I was being double billed for quite a few of the orders. I contacted my provider and asked what was going on. I went over the whole history and pointed out the double billing. They informed me that it was a technical glitch, and they would fix it. They refunded *some* of the money, and I figured that was the end of it. Nothing else happened out of the ordinary for several months, and there was no more double billing.

Lo and behold, all of a sudden I started noticing the double billing again. So I requested refunds for them. They would refund a couple of them but not the rest. When I called them, I was told that the other double billing was over thirty days old and they don't refund anything over thirty days. I couldn't believe it. I started looking over my history from about two months prior, and as I was looking through the history, suddenly another double bill popped up, right in front of my eyes. They were adding even more charges. I caught them going back and adding more double bills in the history that was over thirty days past. It was shocking to sit there and watch it happen right in front of me. They apparently didn't know I was on the site, watching them.

I decided to see if I could catch them, so I started only adding twenty dollars when I needed money to ship a twelve dollar package. The twenty dollars was made available to their account to use but when I checked my bank account later that day, I saw where they had taken out two twenty dollar charges but only gave me use of the one twenty dollar payment. When I called them on it, they lied and said the post office had taken it. I checked, but the post office hadn't. I have documented proof of $750 that they took, and that was only after I caught them. No telling how many thousands they have taken over the years. That 5 percent I was saving by shipping online ended up costing me thousands—definitely no bargain.

I contacted the Better Business Bureau in Silicon Valley where they are located, and since this is basically mail fraud, I also contacted the fraud department of the post office. No one would investigate it. The point is, if they were doing that to me, a small business, how many billions are they stealing from the thousands of companies using their services? Who would ever suspect that a big company like that would be stealing from us?

I finally went to Pitney Bowes and now use their services, but believe me, I check to be sure the money I put in the account is totally available and nothing is missing. So far, they have been honest. These big corporations can get away with anything, and no one will do a thing about it, and no lawyer will take them on.

This was outright theft. I figure over the years before I caught them, I lost several thousand dollars to them. If you are using them, get someone who can check it out, and be sure they aren't stealing from you too. *Don't trust them!*

The best way to keep track is like this: When you put money in the online shipping company's account, keep track of how much each package you send out costs. When you are told to add more funds to your account, add up the amounts of the packages you have mailed since the last deposit and be sure it equals the amount they are claiming you used up. Keep your eye on your history, and be sure you aren't double billed. If enough of us get together and go after them with a class action suit, perhaps we can get it stopped. But other than that, good luck trying to get anyone to investigate them.

On a final note, when I was using the online mailing service, I had to pay them a monthly service fee. I cancelled the service and changed my bank account number so they can't get into my funds, yet every month they continue to bill me that monthly fee. They now have me up to nearly two hundred dollars in back fees, *after* I cancelled them.

CHAPTER 4

COUNTING THE COST

These are big scams targeted mostly at the elderly. Let's take a look at a few of them to see where the trap is that makes you think it's a good deal.

The production company hires two people who look like a couple but in reality just met for the first time on the set. According to the actors repeating a script, this car company saved them thousands of dollars when their car broke down. They sit in lawn chairs and say, "They saved me three thousand in car repairs; I am so glad I had CarShield," or whatever the name of the company is producing the commercial.

What they are appealing to is the emotions of senior citizens. What is the *biggest fear seniors have*? The loss of independence and mobility. The last thing a senior wants to lose is their car, and since these actors make it sound like you may have that same big bill the actors talk about, you will win, win, win if you get that policy. It appeals to the seniors' fear of not being able to pay the big bill, which will result in the loss of their car. The senior is duped into believing the policy will secure their independence.

I wanted to see how much they would really save me if I bought their insurance. I decided to check their claims, so I called Car Shield, only to find out their insurance would cost me $1416 a year, which is more than my actual car insurance. On top of that, they claim they are providing roadside service, towing, etc., which may already be covered by your regular car insurance. The commercial is worded in such a way to make you feel like it is free and believe your old car will be covered forever as long as you pay your premium. In reality, when your car reaches a certain mileage, they will drop you anyway and you will get *nothing* back for the thousands you paid in. They are counting on you never having that *big* repair bill, because most people don't. I am eighty-four years old, been driving since I was sixteen, and *never*, in all the older and newer cars I have had throughout the years, did I have a major repair with such high costs. With the cost of that insurance, I could have bought my car twice.

They just pick numbers out of the air that are designed to scare you. When I checked, most of the repair bill costs they mention are way overinflated. If you keep that insurance for, say, three years and don't have a breakdown, you will have paid $4,248, and that is what they are counting on. How many times have you or someone you know had that kind of repair every few years that would make that insurance worth the cost? Remember, these are actors getting paid to lie to you so you will buy into the program and make the insurer rich.

I know how they work because when I was in the television industry, I auditioned for a laundry detergent commercial. They didn't care that I didn't use that detergent, only that I made it look like I did.

When my niece smashed up my car, my insurance company, Geico, paid for the repairs, gave us a rental car, and paid the other party damages—far more than what Car Shield would have paid. When my battery failed, Geico sent someone out to get us going and brought the new battery, which was installed at no cost. I had to pay for the new battery, but not the service.

One actor, Mr. Big, gets up there and says, "When the warranty on my car ran out, Car Shield paid the big bill for that major repair." If the warranty just run out, I wonder how old that car could have been? If you have an *old* car like he made it appear, believe me, you haven't had a factory warranty on it for years, as factory warranties drop off at a certain time or mileage. So how old was his car? Even if the factory warranty drops and you get a major repair right away, it can't be that old; you probably just got a lemon. Over time, the premiums will cost you far more than the repairs. Besides, it doesn't cover everything anyway. *Count the cost. Buyer beware!*

Before you buy into these scams, be sure of exactly what your insurer provides: what they actually cover, at what mileage they drop you, and what services overlap your regular car insurance policy. Add up those monthly premiums, figure out what you will be paying, and look back at how many times you have had a major repair. Compare the cost of a major repair, then calculate how much you would have had to pay in premiums to offset the actual repair costs. *Count your cost before jumping into an agreement*, and be sure you really need it. Just because a major film star is promoting it, it doesn't make it real. You don't think they wouldn't lie to you when they are making big bucks to con you into believing the script?

If you have the personal discipline, find out what the premiums for their insurance would be, then open a savings account. You will be amazed at how much that will add up to in time, and if you don't put money into it for one month, you lose nothing. You miss a month of premiums and you lose all you have invested in those companies.

The other commercial that makes me boil is the one for Colonial Penn. The actors come on—again, I say actors being paid to lie and make it sound like this insurance is going to protect your family with final expenses. None of us want to leave our families with bills. I have talked to hundreds of seniors, and it weighs heavy on their hearts, and these crooks know that.

They say you need this insurance because it is *so* affordable—anyone can pay it. Really? Who wouldn't want to protect their family for so little? They make you think you will get a big amount that will really pay for your fourteen thousand dollar funeral bill, plus the bills you may leave your family to pay. They make you believe they will provide for you and give you peace of mind. They have the couple stand up there and say, "My mom didn't have this insurance, and we are still paying those bills"—appealing to your guilt that you would do this to your family.

In reality, you have to pay the premium for six months before it goes into effect. So you pay $59.70 before it is activated, and if you die in the sixth month, your family will get a whopping $650, period, nothing more. You think that is a big help? Think again. That would pay for the funeral notice in the newspaper!

In one year you will pay $119.40, two years $238.80, etc., and if you take out the policy at age fifty, like the commercial recommends you do and you die at sixty-five, you will have paid them $1,701 and your family will still only get $650. In the commercial the actress mother tells her fifty-year-old son that she got the insurance to protect him, so he should get it to protect his family. She then tries to make her son feel guilty, because, after all, he should be able to afford such a small amount to protect his family. After all, she is protecting him.

What they are really hoping is that you will live to be eighty-five, at which time you would have paid them $3,756.30. Since they will not insure anyone over eighty-five, they will drop you and you get nothing back. They keep it all, so if you die at eighty-six or later, your family gets a big *nothing*.

If you really want to help your family, open a savings account and put in ten dollars or so per month, with your inheritors named as beneficiaries. You will save more and provide far more if you live long enough. You can have the bank automatically take out whatever amount you can afford from your checking account—at least that ten dollars a month—and automatically pass it over into a savings account for you. You won't even know it is gone. You will be surprised how fast that will grow over time, and you will have peace of mind, because you now have a little nest egg that won't be going into someone else's pocket.

When you are young and have a young family to provide for, there is always a chance something will happen to one of you. That is the time you take out a reasonable life insurance plan to cover your family, so they won't be destitute at your passing. For us older folk, there are better ways to leave money for our final expenses, mostly getting out of debt.

Again, count the cost before you buy, and look for safer ways to protect your family and your investments. For the average person on Social Security, you can't afford to have some shyster take what little bit you have to live on. To many people, it isn't much, but to some of us, it is huge. These ads all talk about how "affordable" their product or service is. Affordable to whom? They almost make you feel like something is wrong with you if you can't afford it. If you buy into all these sales pitches—nineteen dollars here, ten dollars there, on and on—it really adds up over time. Wouldn't you rather have that in a nest egg for emergencies or for your family that you will not lose, like you would with the so-called insurance policies?

For us older folk, there are better ways to leave money for our final expenses. Getting out of debt is the most important thing you can do to protect those you leave behind. Secondly, you can pay for your funeral ahead of time, like I did with my cremation. It's paid for, and the cost is locked in, so it won't be affected by inflation.

Another thing you have to be careful of as a senior is life insurance. Years ago, my income was basically what sustained us, as my husband had retired and his Social Security didn't cover our expenses. I decided to look into getting a term life insurance policy to pay things off for him, should I die. I contacted AIG to get a $250,000 policy, which would pay off everything and give him funds to live on. I passed the physical with flying colors even though I was in my late sixties. I was pretty naive about things like term life, so I had a talk with the agent to find out what would happen if I survived past the ten-year term. What would happen to the money I had paid in? Again I didn't contact a lawyer but believed the agent who informed me that nothing would be lost as long as I kept up the premiums.

For the term of the policy, the premium was only $199 a month, so I assumed that once the term was up I would still just go on paying the existing premium of $199. I made sure those payments were always in on time, which over the years added up to twenty-three thousand dollars.

When the ten years was up, they contacted me to see if I wanted to continue to keep the policy or not. When I said sure, I can afford that $199 a month, the agent quickly said, "Oh no, your premium changes. In order to keep the policy, your premium would go to $2,300 per month."

I was shocked. I realized the original agent knew what was going to happen but failed to warn me that it would go up. He had made it sound like nothing would change, just keep paying as usual. When I tried to negotiate something or get some of my money back the agent basically laughed at me and told me my money belonged to them now. There were no returns whatsoever. They got to keep the twenty-three thousand dollars; I was just out the money. You wonder how I could have been so stupid? Well chalk it up to trusting without knowing the facts, which of course, they weren't about to tell me. I should have known better, because they had cheated me before.

I had a car insurance with AIG for several years before the above incident. Because of my good driving record, I had a very low, locked-in rate. They contacted me one day to inform me that they wanted to increase the rate but had to have me agree to it before they could. I told them no, I don't have accidents and never had, so I wanted to keep the low rate. This was back before everyone had computers and could pay online, so I always made sure my premium check got into their office on time.

I just forgot about the conversation and went on about building my new business. I sent in my next check, which was never returned. When the third month rolled around they finally contacted me to tell me to stop sending checks, as I had not been insured by them for at least three months. They just claimed they had never received my first checks, so with *no* warning, they had cancelled my insurance.

I thought they were a reputable company, but to my horror, I found out differently. I had been driving around with no insurance for three months, unbeknownst to me. I was freaked. They also informed me that if I wanted my insurance back, I would now have to pay the higher premium that I had refused to accept earlier. I realized they had done this on purpose, never warning me they were about to cancel my insurance, so that they could get me off their old fixed rate. It was a dirty trick.

Now I had to get insurance immediately somewhere else. And because I had been driving with no insurance for three months, I now had to pay a penalty of a higher rate for over two years, even though it had only lapsed for two months, I hadn't known it, and it was no fault of mine. I was stuck. The interesting thing is that a month later, they returned my checks they claimed they had never received, which caused the cancellation in the first place. It was in their envelope, so I knew they had opened my envelopes to them and held on to the checks to trick me. It just feels like everywhere you turn, somebody is going to screw you one way or another.

Life insurance will do that too. I believed the commercials for Senior Life Insurance Company that say they will help seniors get such a good rate to cover final expenses, etc. I have a lot of animals, and at the time I took out the policy with Senior Life, my husband was still alive. I was trying to be sure he had enough money to take care of our show dogs and our other pets, should I pass away before him. I thought I was taking out an eight thousand dollar policy for which I had I paid sixty-three dollars a month. I wanted to be sure I didn't miss a payment, so I had it automatically taken out. I paid into it for over ten years.

Over the years my husband and a lot of my dogs died, but I still had a lot of older champions my heirs would need to care for. I contacted Senior Life to see if my policy would ever be paid up. They informed me that the policy would only be paid up when I reached one hundred years of age and only if I kept up the premiums until then. Since I am eighty-four, if I lived to one hundred, I would have paid them a total over all the years of a whopping $19,144, and still my heirs would only get eight thousand dollars? They also informed me that I didn't have an eight-thousand-dollar policy like I thought but only had a six-thousand-dollar policy.

I realized what a mistake I had made, so I cashed in my policy and received a whopping $1,800 back, and they got to keep the rest—$5,760. That money would be safely in a savings account had I done it right. Now I have a special insurance saving account that is growing rapidly. Even though savings accounts pay low interest, it is still a better deal than throwing money at that policy. At least if I skip a month, I don't lose anything, like I would have had I missed one month's payment.

You sure have to be careful when you hear a commercial that says, "It is only $14.95, money-back guarantee." They don't tell you that that money is a fee so you can try the product they are advertising, but is not the price of the product. I called about an air-brush system, as it looked like a neat thing to apply makeup. I figured a little well-applied paint on my old face wouldn't hurt, so I called them. I wanted to be sure there were no surprises and no additional charges.

They kept evading my questions trying to make me look like a fool, because how could I put a price like $14.95 on my looks? I wouldn't place the order until they gave me the real price, which turned out to be $157 to $300 for that device. The $14.95 was extra just to try it out, and if I didn't return it within thirty days, they would instantly suck the full purchase price from the same credit card.

They don't tell you that the thirty days starts at the time you place the order, not when you receive the merchandise. By the time you get the product, at least seven days has already gone by, if they get it out quickly. Since it has to be returned within thirty days, you basically only have a week or two at the most to try it out before you have to get it in the mail back to them. These things all look good, but almost always there is a hitch. I love their theme song, "If I Could Turn Back Time," which is what they are claiming their makeup will do for you. You can paint it, baby, but turning back time just ain't gonna happen.

Another one they use commonly is, "Wow, you need to try this for free—two free bottles." This one also means that at the end of the thirty-day trial they will suck out the full price for the product. I recently bit into that one; you would think by now I would know better.

A friend has trouble sleeping, so I contacted Relaxium Sleep. I trusted a well-known Christian I saw on a commercial for them; after all, he wouldn't lie, because he's a Godly man. He said the product starts working the first night. He said it is risk free, and then at the end of the commercial he says they believe the product will work so well, they are giving away a thousand bottles. It leaves you thinking that you can call and order that one free-trial bottle.

I ordered that one free bottle for her to try, or so I thought. I didn't think much about it until it arrived with two bottles in the package. There wasn't any paperwork in the bag informing me that if I didn't return this within thirty days (in reality, two weeks) I would have to pay full price for them. I gave my friend one bottle to see if it helped. Because the people in the commercial claimed that it worked the very first night, we expected her to get immediate results too. For the first few nights it helped her fall asleep faster but didn't help her sleep longer, and when she took another pill after waking up, the second one didn't work. I didn't do anything about sending it back, because I thought it was a free bottle.

When I called to order it, the agent on the phone did not emphasize or make clear that if I kept it, it was no longer a free bottle or free trial. At the end of thirty days, I suddenly found $118 taken out of my account. I called them to find out what happened to that free trial, only to be informed that we were in reality just trying it for free, but if we kept the product, it wasn't free. Because I hadn't returned it, I now had to pay the full price. After quite a discussion, I made it clear that that is not what the ad said nor was that made clear to me when I ordered the product. At least they gave me half of the money back, but I was still out fifty-nine dollars. They wouldn't even let me send back the unopened bottle; they said I should keep it, because sometimes it takes months of use before it works. Total deception and the total opposite of what the commercial indicated.

I just hope that Godly man doesn't know how the company is roping people in like they did me. I don't even remember ordering two. If he knows, then shame on him. As the saying goes, "There's no fool like an old fool."

These companies are always spouting some new gimmick to get you. I love the new one: In order to get you to hurry up and buy, they are now advertising that you must get it right now. Only two to a customer or whatever limit they put on it. Because of the rise in costs, we are shutting down production. Get yours quickly before they are all gone.

Now, one after the other, companies are adding that line to their promo. If they are so limited, how can they afford the expensive advertisements to sell them? They are taking advantage of and using inflation as an excuse to make you believe they are going out of business so you will rush in and grab what is left. They remind me of the old toilet paper problem during the early pandemic days.

One of the things that really scare me is the fact that this government administration is pushing car makers to go strictly with electric cars and not even make gas engines anymore. The batteries in those cars only last a couple of years, which have to be replaced to the tune of five thousand dollars. How many average working households can afford that? Besides, what if the power goes down or the power grid has a problem for a week like it did during the storms last year? You won't go anywhere because you may have to charge the car, and there is no place to get electricity. This is just another way for the government to control you. In California, the governor is telling people *not* to charge their electric cars because there is too much drain on the power grid. So now how do they get around?

By the way, a lot of those charging stations are powered by diesel generators, and a lot of the power is produced by coal-powered plants. Both sources produce air pollution, so how do electric cars help the environment? Give me my gas car. I'll worry about the air another way.

Since I have had so much pulled on me and see so much crookedness happen, I now watch my accounts carefully. Our telephone company used to provide cable service for our TV. It began to cost them more than they could charge us, so we had to look for service elsewhere. My favorite channel is MeTV, with all the old programs on it that I know and love. I guess it creates a lot of nostalgia, because I know so many of those actors when I was in the industry doing talk shows all over the world. The only provider that carried that channel was Dish, so I went to them.

For the first few months my charge was one price, eighty dollars for the channels I wanted. That was fine, but at the end of the three months I started seeing additional charges. When I called them, they informed me that the charge was for the movie channels, which I never requested and never watched anyway. Repeatedly, I had to call and stop them. I informed them that they were to add *nothing*, and I emphasized *nothing*, to my bill. I didn't want anything else, just what I had. The salesperson tried to make me feel stupid because I didn't take advantage of "such a bargain."

Again and again they kept contacting me, telling me they had a bargain for me if I would take their cell phone service. I have been with AT&T since 1980. They have been wonderful to me in *every* way and I kept telling Dish, no, leave me alone.

On September 12, 2022, I opened my bank account only to find another charge to my account for eleven dollars. When I called to ask Dish what that was for, they informed me that they had just given me a three-month free trial for an insurance to cover any repairs to the equipment I was renting from them. If anything went wrong and I didn't keep the protection plan, I would have to pay a ninety-dollar service charge to have someone come out and repair *their* equipment—their box and dish I was already paying a rental fee to use. I couldn't believe it. Why should I pay rent on their equipment and then pay to have it repaired should it break down? In less than nine months I would have paid in the same as a service fee. Why would I do that? Were they planning on their equipment going down so they could get more money out of me? Or were they just counting on the fact that I would be paying them $132 a year for a possible ninety dollar repair that I would probably not even need. This would give them a nice fat bundle of money they would pocket on top of the monthly rental fee.

There was no way I was going to rent something and then pay the repairs on it. That is like renting an apartment and then if a pipe leaks you have to pay the landlord to fix it. That is all part of the rental. Anything to get an extra buck out of you. It adds up over a period of time. If their equipment breaks down, they had better repair it, or I will see them in small claims court or find another provider. There are a lot of them out there looking to serve you. Sadly, the reason I even went with this company in the first place was to get MeTV, which they have now dropped and is no longer available through any server.

There is one more commercial out there that gives me a chuckle when I see it. It starts out with an actor and actress sitting on a couch. They can't be older than their late forties. They are advertising a company that provides personal incontinent pads and pants. This company claims they keep your business private and save you a lot of money if you have Medicare. At the end of the commercial, she says, "They save us hundreds of dollars each month."

What? Are you kidding me? Who in the world uses so many diapers or pads that cost retail up to maybe twelve dollars for a box of thirty pads, that it would save you hundreds of dollars each month? You would have to be using a truckload worth thousands of dollars to save hundreds. They must be supplying the neighborhood or a nursing home. They didn't look like they were old enough to even be on Medicare.

Oops, either the writer wrote the wrong script and didn't understand what incontinence products were or the actress didn't understand what was in the script and improvised. Or perhaps whoever edited the finished ad didn't understand what was being said. Pretty funny and makes me laugh to see how stupid it is. I wonder if anyone else caught it?

CHAPTER 5

PREDATORY LENDING AND OTHER BANK TRICKS TO GET YOUR MONEY

This chapter will tell you why you must always follow these four rules when dealing with banks.

Never sign *any* document when you are tired, under stress, or going through grief.

Never use your property or home as security for a loan.

Most important of all, go home, sleep on it a few days and pray about your decision. God has promised us that the Holy Spirit will give us wisdom if we just ask. James 1:5: "If any of you lacks wisdom, let him ask of God who gives generously to all, and it will be given to you."

If you don't have complete peace about it, don't do it. God knows what is going to happen, and He wants to protect you from any hidden traps. If you have even the slightest feeling of uneasiness, that is the Holy Spirit giving you a check: "Don't do it."

This chapter will make clear why I have made the above statements.

It was a chilly day in late October. I had been home dealing with problems with my business, which was struggling, and a myriad of other situations. I was in a hurry to get back to the hospital to be with my beloved husband who was fighting for his life. I was staying in my motor home outside the hospital and barely left his side for nearly two months. I was exhausted. Needless to say, I was stressed, not on a scale of one to ten, but off the chart altogether. I knew I had a loan payment due at my bank where I had been doing all my business for several years, so I decided to make a quick stop at the Clackamas branch to make the payment. Just one more thing out of the way.

One of the bank officers came over to help me because the tellers were all busy. He took a few minutes to look up my loan while going *hmm* and looking at me carefully. He said, "You know you are paying too high an interest rate of 13 percent. If you can take a few minutes, I can help you cut that to 2 percent. I really want to help you." I was shocked and lulled into believing him; he seemed so kind and helpful. Never before have I had a banker try to lower an interest rate. As we walked over to his cubicle, I was thinking, "Wow, this bank really cares about their people!"

As we sat down, he proceeded to tell me if I would consolidate my bills and use my property as collateral, I could get a loan with them for 2 percent for the life of the loan. I thought, "That would save me a lot of money." I was paying for my motor home at 4.5 percent and had a couple of credit cards I had foolishly run the balances up on at over 13 percent interest. His proposal would save me thousands and I'd have only one monthly payment to worry about. I thought he was really trying to help me, so I bought the deal hook, line, and sinker. Where do I sign up? We did the paperwork, and off I went to the hospital feeling pretty good about what had just happened.

When the document came for me to sign the final papers, I looked at the ten pages of legalese, which, in my rush to get back to the hospital, I hadn't taken the time to read. I knew I wouldn't understand it anyway, and since this gentleman was so caring and helpful, I trusted him. I had signed and left. I relied on my own understanding and emotions instead of asking God to guide me. If I had, I wouldn't be in this mess I was in now, because He would have stopped me. Even though the banker had promised me 2 percent for the life of the loan, the bank had slipped a clause down on page six or seven in one small sentence: *Interest only for fifteen years*. I didn't catch it.

I have since learned that what they did is a common practice with many banks and lenders. They agree to one thing but then slip in other clauses where you won't find them, like they did with me. They also slipped in the 2 percent for just two years, then it went to a variable rate, not a fixed rate like the banker promised. The only way you can prevent them from slipping something in is to take the document to a lawyer and when they okay it, do not let that document out of your hands until it is signed with a notary. This will prevent the bank from changing anything, like they will if they get their hands on the document before you sign it.

I really didn't pay attention to bills when they came into my house because I have everything written down with the payment amounts and their due date. I would just grab the checkbook and head to the bank to make that payment or send it in, far in advance, so it was never late. This went on for a couple of years until one day I went into the bank to find out why the payment slip showed the payment doubled. What a shock when the banker looked at my loan and informed me that down on page three or so it said that the interest was 2 percent for two years then it went to variable. Oh my, now I was paying 7 percent for a loan that had only been 4.5 percent at the previous bank. It was hidden in the middle of a paragraph, which I never caught. I found out that "banker" who was so nice had conned me into a bad deal. He caught me at my most vulnerable time and lied to me, and I stupidly bought the lie. He must have gotten a nice bonus for conning me into signing. He knew I would make the payments, which seemed so much lower at the time, because I don't want to lose my property. This was just the first step in the saga.

The bank informed me one day that I could no longer make the payment at the bank, but had to do it online. Now I was in my early seventies and not very computer savvy, so I got on the phone with their online tech and proceeded to set up the online payments. As we were doing so, the tech made the comment, "I have never seen a loan like this with interest only for fifteen years." I was shocked by his comment, only to learn that all the money I had been paying for the past ten years hadn't only gone up from 2 percent to a variable rate but also that only about five dollars of the hundreds I spent every month was going toward the principle. I couldn't believe my ears. What kind of mess had I gotten into!!!

In over ten years I had only paid about a thousand dollars on the principle of the $105,000 consolidation loan. I still owed $104,000, so I went to the FDIC, the organization that oversees banking practices, and complained. They forwarded my complaint to the head of that bank, who refused to do anything. They said I signed it, so it was binding. They weren't even willing to make any kind of compromise and apply any of that interest to the loan.

At the time I signed the papers, my property was worth $300,000 but is now worth $650,000. They are counting on the fact that I am getting older and will die, so they will get my property at a fat profit. Now at eighty-four years of age when my medical and living expenses have gone way up, my payments have jumped from a couple hundred a month to over a thousand. It is no wonder I have to still work full time, or they will take my property and I would be out on the street.

What they did is called *predatory lending*, and I have found other seniors who have had the same thing happen to them. This is worse than usury, which was made illegal several years ago, because the banks were charging too high an interest rate. This is the modern version of a loan shark. Seems it is a fairly common practice of many banks, not just mine. Needless to say, I took my business to another bank as soon as I learned what they were doing.

I tried to get an attorney, but no attorney or judge will take on a bank, no matter how much you offer them or how right you are. The big lesson I learned from this is never sign a document without having a lawyer read it first. Only the lawyers know the tricks and what the document is really saying. I was too trusting, which is what many of us older folk tend to do when we are undergoing the loss of spouses, our friends dying, or when illness takes our energy and our social security, etcetera. At the time I signed the document, I couldn't afford a lawyer and was too stressed to think straight. Besides, I trusted that "sweet" banker.

Had I not signed that agreement, all those loans would have been paid off years ago, but instead, after eighteen years of payments, I still owe the same amount I originally borrowed. I figured out that I have paid the bank nearly ninety thousand in interest and still have the same debt. What the banks are counting on is the fact that you will pay that loan even though it involves higher costs at a time when you really can't afford it, because if you don't, you will lose your home. If you can't pay, then they own your property, which will be more valuable than when you first took out the loan. Predatory lending should be outlawed.

WHERE CAN YOU FIND HELP, EVEN IF YOU CAN'T AFFORD IT?

Now I know there are places to go and get the financial help to get a lawyer. I have learned that most senior centers all over the country have attorney's that come to the center and give seniors a thirty-minute free consultation. That would have been long enough for a lawyer to have caught the predatory lending and the hidden mess about the interest. He would have told me the banker had lied to me to rope me into getting him a bonus.

I have also learned that you can call your state bar and get help. There are lawyers available to help with simple advice or go over a document pro bono for seniors who can't afford legal counsel. *Pro bono* means that the lawyer doesn't charge you—so there are avenues you can take to protect yourself. Sad to say, banks are not out there to help you but to make money for themselves at your expense. They know we will do anything—go without food, medical care or whatever—to make that inflated payment so we don't lose our home.

All of this from one of the top banks in America that claims, "We make your dreams come true. Come bank with us." Yes, they make your dreams come true—the ones we call nightmares.

Get help, and don't sign any document until you get legal advice. That is more important than ever, because we don't think as clearly as we did when we were younger and besides, who reads all ten pages of that legalese? Only a lawyer; so protect yourself. Even if you have to pay for a one-time lawyer to look over the document, that $125 one-hour fee will save you thousands. At the time, I was just too overwhelmed to stop and think it through. Such an important action at the time could have saved me a lot of heartache and stress. If I had just remembered that I have a God who knows more than I do, who would have stopped me if I had just asked Him.

One other thing you have to watch out for is the tricks some of the banks pull to cheat you out of more of your money. I also had a small loan with another major bank. I always sent the payment in early to avoid late fees, only to have them calling all three of my phones on the due date telling me my payment was late and I would have a late fee. I was shocked as I had sent the payment to their loan department in Arizona at least a week early along with the payment and due date accompanying the check.

To avoid the problem the next month, I tried sending it in two weeks early. To my surprise, they applied the payment as an extra payment to the previous month.

When I confronted them, I was told that since it came in early they just applied it to the month they were receiving it. They did this in spite of the fact that it had the payment slip in the envelope that stated it was for the payment due in a week. They said I still owed for the following payment, which now carried a late fee.

The harassment was awful. Three calls a day and a letter every day. It went on for days like that, so I decided to avoid the mail and go to the local branch to make the payment. I made sure I paid it was exactly on the due date so there would be no question as to when the payment was made. That didn't stop them from harassing me. When I called them on the fact that it was paid on the due date at the branch, I was informed that since I made it at the branch, it didn't arrive at their facility in Arizona for at least three days, therefore it was late.

I talked to a friend of mine who worked in their loan payment processing department to see if there was anything I could do to get this mess under control. She informed me she had quit. She said the bank made her hold the payments on her desk until they became late, claiming to the customer the check didn't arrive on time. Then they could charge the borrower the late fees on that loan. She couldn't stand being so dishonest and hurting people like that, so she quit.

On other days I would go into the branch to make a deposit to my checking account to be sure some small checks I had written were covered if they happened to come in early. Suddenly I started noticing a lot of overdraft fees, so I went to the bank again to find out what was going on. I found out the bank was holding my deposit for a couple of days but went ahead and paid the checks that came in, causing overdraft fees on every one of them. The teller told me that holding deposits for a few days was the policy of the bank. Such dishonesty from what is considered one of the top banks in the country!

The late fees and harassment went on, and finally I knew I had to get out of there, so I went to a group that helped people with credit problems. When I explained what was going on, I never told them what bank it was, but they laughed and said, "Oh, you must be with . . ." and they named my bank. They had been helping a lot of people get out of there, because they were having the same problems I experienced. I don't know if they are still doing that, but they sure put me through hell and cost me a lot of money. How do you prevent this kind of stress?

Whenever you apply for a loan or a credit card, be sure you can pay it online before 5 p.m. on the due date so the payment will be credited on that day. Print out the page that says it was paid on that day and hold onto that receipt. The only time you pay early is when you want an extra payment applied to the principle, but make your payment on—and I stress, on— the due date. If you don't do it online, make sure you take it into the branch and make sure they credit it that day and not when it arrives at the processing center. Get a receipt. I have found that most banks will now transfer payments electronically, so they are credited that day. Get the receipt in hard copy before you leave the branch to be sure that they are crediting your account immediately. Be aware and make sure before you sign that loan or take out that credit card, that you have all terms in writing. Know exactly how your account is credited. I ran into a similar problem with the bank through Costco and just closed the account. Not worth the stress.

My husband and I loved to travel a great deal in the motor home. We went to Camping World to get some repairs, and while there we were approached by a salesperson about a camping membership that would "save us a lot of money." We looked at the program that said we could stay at the campgrounds all over the United States for free, so since we knew we would use it, we put down the two thousand dollars on our Washington Mutual Bank credit card.

They only gave us a receipt and told us we would be receiving our documents and locations of the campgrounds in a few days via the mail. RV parks at that time were charging ten to twenty-five dollars a night with full hookups. As much as we traveled, it was a good deal. A few days later we received the packet of campground locations. To our surprise it wasn't anything like they had told us. We could only go to the campgrounds in their system, which just happened to be in the most out-of-the-way, far-off-the-beaten-path locations—places we never went. When we tried to stay at the only one we could find in Oregon, we found out that our membership let us in, but we still had to pay ten dollars a night.

We were furious, as that was not what we were told in the meeting. So since we weren't getting what we paid for, we went back to Washington Mutual Bank and told them what happened. They were wonderful, because they recognized that we had been scammed; so they refunded the charges we had paid, and we went on our way thinking it was all taken care of.

Everything seemed to be settled until a few months later, when the biggest bank in the United States, bought out Washington Mutual. They contacted me to inform me that they were going to reinstate the two thousand dollar charge to Camping World. I informed them in writing that it was an illegal charge, and they were not to give them the money. No bank can charge your credit card without your permission, and I knew that if they did, I had grounds to sue them. They did it anyway—reinstated the two thousand dollars and billed me for it.

After months of harassment, calls and letters of demand by that new bank, I finally talked to a friend of mine who is a retired superior court judge and asked him what I could do. He told me to sue them, because what they had done was definitely illegal. I couldn't find a lawyer that would take on a bank so with my judge friend's help, I made out my own papers and served the bank.

When we finally got to court, I sat there watching the judge listen to several people who had represented themselves only to watch him throw them *all* out of court and tell them they didn't have their papers right. They needed to go get a lawyer. By the time it was my turn I could see the handwriting on the wall and sure enough, he threw my case out of court and told me to get an attorney because the papers were wrong. Really? Papers filled out with the help of a superior court judge were wrong?

As I walked out of the court room, the lawyer who worked for the bank I was suing, stopped me and said, "You have a legitimate case against them, and you should have been awarded a large sum of money for what they did. But that is why I get paid five hundred dollars an hour to stop you." With high paid lawyers and crooked judges who are working with their lawyer buddies to make people hire them, I knew I was screwed.

I tried for months to get an attorney, but none of them would take on a bank. I finally found one, but all he did was call me on the phone and run up my bill over nonsense questions that I had already answered. He did that until he used up all my $1500 retainer. When I couldn't come up with a lot more money, he told me I couldn't win anyway and dropped me. I was furious and demanded my retainer back. I informed him that if I didn't get my full retainer back I would take him to the state attorney board and tell them how he just ran up my calls and did nothing for me. It was so obvious he was just after what he could get and never intended to do anything. Thankfully, it worked, and I got my full retainer back.

I know of a military family where the husband was deployed to Iraq. His house was paid off before he left, so he felt secure that his family was safe. While he was overseas, a local bank claimed that the soldier owed a mortgage, and because the family hadn't been making the payments, the bank was foreclosing on them. The bank's papers were not legal, and when the wife went to court to fight it, she had the papers to prove the house was paid off. It didn't matter to the judge; he just gave the home to the bank, and they were left homeless. What a crooked judge who would treat the military men on deployment like that and abuse his family. The judges are ruthless. They seem to work for the banks and help to fatten the pockets of the lawyers no matter how right you are.

One of the biggest scams going now is the reverse mortgage scheme. They know how to rope you into it by using actors who get paid to stand up there on screen and tell you what the bank wants to you hear. They are repeating the script they were given. These actors are always the ones people love because they play parts of good guys and are handsome like Tom Selleck. They can stand up there and con you with sweet words, because these are acting jobs, and how would someone wealthy like Selleck, who would never have to take out a reverse mortgage, know what really goes on? He says in the commercial, "The bank isn't interested in owning your home." Wrong, Tom; they are. If you are in the clutches of a bank, you stand to lose everything, so tread with caution no matter who tells you that you are safe. Get everything in writing. The commercials make you believe that even if you use up your equity, you will be able to stay in your home that you "love". Not true.

Let me share a couple of experiences I know of, such as one case right here in Portland, Oregon. A lady took out a reverse mortgage on her home that had a lot of equity. Long before the equity was used up, the city came and took her property as public domain. (They can force you out when they declare that the property is needed for the public good.) Since the bank basically owned the house because of the reverse mortgage loan and even though she still had a lot of equity available, the city paid the bank for the property, and the bank kept every penny. She was out on the street with nothing. They didn't even pay her the balance of what she still had coming.

I had a very good friend whose sister owned a valuable piece of property in California. She had quite a bit of equity in her home, so she thought life would be easier with a reverse mortgage. She lived long enough to use up all her equity, and when the bank contacted her, she was told she had to get another full mortgage, pay all the closing costs, and pay the higher market value for the property if she wanted to stay in her home. She had spent all she had and the bank ended up with her home at a big profit.

The ads make you think you can stay in your home forever, even if you use up all the equity, but as these people found out, that is not true. You have to buy it back or you are evicted. Pretty good deal for the bank, because they now own her place, which is worth much more now than it was when she took out the reverse mortgage. Good deal for them; bad deal for her.

I am so grateful I know Jesus and have the Holy Spirit to guide me. Before I met the people who had lost everything due to their reverse mortgages, I had been looking into it for myself. It all sounded so good, and Tom Selleck wouldn't lie to me, would he? I have learned not to jump into anything anymore, especially when it comes to finances. So I spent a lot of time in prayer, asking the Holy Spirit what to do. Over and over He emphatically told me, *no*, don't do it. It was after I decided to obey that I learned of the situations above. I thank Him every day for protecting me. Sad to say, banks are not out there to help you but to make money for themselves at your expense.

The last item I want to warn you about is scams on the TV and Internet. I opened my email one day and found an ad that appeared to be from Walmart. It said that I had earned the opportunity from my Walmart credit card to receive a free gift if I would just check out the offers. I opened it and looked down the list and found a dash camera, very small, that was on sale for only $17.95. Well, when I see the word *sale*, I expect to purchase that item at that price, not just be paying to try it out. I stupidly didn't ask God first; I thought it was a good deal. Walmart wouldn't cheat me, or so I thought. I gave them my bank card and purchased it. It arrived a few days later in a small box but with no paperwork.

Well, again, shock. In two weeks I found an added charge from the same people for another $79.95. When I called my credit union, I told them it was a fraudulent charge; I never authorized it.

This credit union had been wonderful to me in the past and really had helped me, so I trusted them to do the right thing. The charge was tentatively removed while they investigated. About a week later, they called me and told me what the seller had said. The seller lied and told them a piece of paper came with the camera telling me that if I kept it, I would be charged another $79.95, and because I hadn't sent it back, I owed the money. I informed the credit union that I had received no paperwork with the camera or at any other time. When I asked the credit union if they had received a copy of the so called contract, they said no, but the vendor told them that they had sent it.

I had been a customer in that credit union for years, paid off a car loan and a motor home loan, and had all my accounts with them, so I felt they should trust me rather than a stranger over the phone who had a lot to gain. No, they listened to the vendor and gave them the $79.95 back with no proof whatsoever that the charge was legitimate. I was furious.

I found the telephone numbers listed on the seller's website and the numbers the credit union had called when they spoke to them. I was going to call that company and complain personally, only to find out they had disconnected all their phones and taken down their website right after the credit union had talked to them. It was then that I realized they weren't from Walmart but had used that store's logo, as many of the crooks are now doing to con you into believing it is a legitimate sale.

I then informed my credit union that these were crooks, as legitimate businesses don't vanish off the face of the earth when questioned. That proved they were crooks and had no right to my money. The scammers obviously knew they were getting caught so disconnected everything and ran. In spite of all this proof showing they were crooks and scammers, I couldn't believe the credit union representative when he said, "Well, we aren't going to get your money back. You gave them your credit card; therefore, they could take the money, and we will not help you." Needless to say, I had a new account in another credit union in just a few days. I am very careful not to use my card unless it is proven to be a legitimate charge with a legitimate company.

You have to be *so* careful. Ask anyone you deal with on the phone or Internet *before you give them your card number* if there is a membership tacked to the purchase. Are they going to take out more money if something isn't stopped within a certain time? Be sure you are dealing with legitimate companies, not some new person you never heard of before. Call the company they claim to represent to be sure the person you are dealing with is really their representative and that the sale is legitimate. Get the exact terms before you make the purchase or agreement.

Once you get hooked, the only way you can stop these people is to have your credit or debit card changed so they can't get into your accounts, or many of them will keep sucking money out each month. Be careful. Find out the details of what you think you are buying, and if it seems like a great deal, it probably isn't. Great deals usually turn out to be bad deals. You get something for free as a trial, then they hit you. And since the bank says you gave them the card, it implies they are free to charge it again. You are stuck with other charges until you change your card.

Are you using a bank card that pays you rewards money back if you use it? Think again—the bank doesn't give you anything. When you use those rewards cards, the bank charges the merchant a higher rate to process them. The merchant then has to raise the cost of their goods to offset those extra charges. It is not a win-win situation, but a lose-lose all the way around.

CHAPTER 6

LEGAL AFFAIRS

This chapter is a bit hard to write because there are some realities every one of us needs to face. The first thing I want to talk about is a *will*. That isn't an option; it is imperative. The best of families may have good intentions, but when you are gone without a will, two things happen. The state steps in, which is something you don't want to happen, or family members start fighting over who gets what. You think it would never happen to your family members, but it is all too common. Greed raises its ugly head, and they go at it over who gets the cups, napkins, etc.

The other thing I have done since I am eighty-four is to put the names on the backs of things, naming who I want to have that particular item that is precious to me. The rest of it, I don't care if it goes to the Salvation Army or preferably some needy family. It is the best way I know of to avoid all family conflict. Since I am nearing the time when I will be going home to be with the Lord, I have decided to give some of my most cherished things to certain family members now to avoid future problems. I am getting rid of everything I haven't used or even remembered I had for the past two years. I don't want that burden left for my family to clean out my house of needless stuff, my treasures that will mean nothing to them.

I tell everyone now that I don't need anything for Christmas, just their love and presence is enough. If they still insist, then a gift certificate to my favorite restaurant or grocery store would be appreciated. My parents' house was so full of stuff, things she was already getting rid of because there wasn't enough room to store it. One Christmas when I was visiting, I couldn't believe my nephews and nieces brought them sets of glasses and other dishes. Poor thing, I thought my mother was going to faint. Food, a dinner out, or a grocery certificate would have meant *so* much more to her. Just more stuff she had to dispose of.

When I was young, I used to give them certificates they could redeem anytime, and they loved it. They would say, "I will do the dishes after dinner for a week," "I will do the laundry this week," or "I will clean the house for two weeks." One was a gift certificate for a date-night out for mom and dad to go to dinner and a movie, redeemable when they wanted to go, etc. That also works both ways. You can give your son or daughter a free babysitting evening, so the frazzled parents can enjoy a date without the kids. Those things mean more than a new set of glasses or plates or the fiftieth tie for dad.

POWER OF ATTORNEY

As we age, it is important to name someone to handle your affairs should you become incapacitated, but oh you better make sure of what you are doing. This is where you definitely need a lawyer to help you. You would never think anyone would do what they do, but greed is a strange bedfellow. I will give you an example of a few cases I have observed.

The first one is that of a retired professional who had developed cancer. The disease weakened him greatly. He was lonely, so he started spending a lot of time on the Internet and got caught in one of the scams where someone pretended to be a pastor who needed money for his church. While he had a lot of possessions, he did pretty much empty his bank account by sending cash to the scammers. His son found out what he was doing, so since he had given him power of attorney, he stepped in. The elder man was too weak to fight him.

The first thing he did was take his beloved pets that he doted on and had them put down right in front of him because he didn't want to be bothered with their care. Then he cleaned out his father's house and had a truck haul all his belongings to the dump, saying it was all junk. He didn't care that some of the things he threw away belonged to his father's friend. Everything that meant anything to his father was gone.

He then remodeled his father's garage and parked him in it with nothing but bare necessities. I am not sure why the senior wasn't better prepared, having been a professional, but it was too late, and he didn't have the strength to stop his son. Who would expect their child to do what he did? As a further insult, he barred all family members from visiting. That should have been a red flag that something was radically wrong, and the family members should have gone to the authorities about their suspicion of elder abuse. Sadly, they didn't.

It was obvious he didn't want any of his inheritance to be spent on animal food and care and didn't want any relatives to observe the terrible conditions in which he had imprisoned his father. This poor man had apparently given the wrong person power of attorney, but he should have kept control of his estate until his passing. What a sad ending to such a productive life.

I know another case where a man gave his child power of attorney. The son hated his step-mother, so he took the nice inheritance his dad had received, paid off his home, bought a new car, etc. The dad got none of it, which forced him and his wife to live in poverty until the wife became ill and died. The dad was then basically put out on the street without even the money to pay the rent on his apartment. Once the wife died the son finally paid his father's rent for a couple of months, but there was no promise of his father getting his money back.

Another friend of mine who lives quite far from me has a mom with a debilitating disease that will take her within the next couple of years. For the sake of clarity, I will call her Betty (not her real name, but I want to protect her privacy). Betty is in her eighties and has a great deal of trouble getting around. My friend took care of her and her old dog, 24/7. My friend knew how much his mother loved going places, so he took her out for adventures and long walks trying to make her last days productive and full. I know them both very well, spent many evenings with them, having fun and meals together. I know that the way my friend was keeping his mom active is exactly how Betty wanted to live out her days.

Unfortunately, it seems Betty gave an in-law power of attorney, and one of the first things they did was lock my friend out and deny him visiting privileges with his own mother. They then hired an unfeeling caregiver at a much higher wage who proceeded to lock Betty out of the bathroom. They made her use a potty chair, which made her feel even more humiliated. I know how she feels because I know her so well. And on and on the abuse goes from that family.

The worst thing that in-law did was to pretty well clean out several hundred thousand dollars from Betty's bank account and put it in an IRA, which Betty can't touch until she is in her nineties. With her advanced disease, she will never make it to her nineties, so the in-law will get to pocket all that money. This maneuver didn't leave Betty enough money to buy her medications for a while, a further humiliation.

My friend has tried everything to get access to his mother and take care of her but can't afford the lawyer to fight for her. He sits home and cries for his mom, and Betty lays in a bare, nine by twelve room, alone, in a foster-care home, grieving. Betty has contacted my friend several times begging him to come and help her escape, but sadly, that is impossible. She isn't even allowed to use the phone to call out and can't even receive calls from her own sister.

Everything that was dear to Betty when they moved her from her cottage was hauled off to the dump by her in-laws. All her belongings that had any meaning to her are gone. Obviously, she gave the wrong person power of attorney.

I know of another case in Ohio where a married man met a single woman and left his family to be with her. He obtained power of attorney over his elderly mom, moved her to a nursing home, emptied her bank accounts, and moved to Florida where he spent it all. This left his mom in a nursing home with nothing.

I could give you case after case that is just a repeat of similar circumstances but could count on one hand those I know of where the family cared for their loved one until they died. When I was young, we never thought of getting rid of family; it was nearly unheard of. We just took care of them when they could no longer care for themselves, but this generation is the throwaway generation. Park them in an assisted living and go on with your life.

To avoid anyone doing to me what has happened to people I mentioned above, I have appointed power of attorney to two different people. They know my wishes exactly, and I know there is a balance there, so they can keep each other from doing the wrong thing for the wrong reasons.

The only time I recommend an assisted living / retirement facility is when a person is pretty much alone and needs minimal care. At least most of the places provide wonderful meals, help cleaning their room, and some allow your pet, so you aren't alone. You have plenty of people to socialize with, you never even have to eat alone. Some facilities even have swimming pools to exercise in.

If you have family who love you and will provide a place for you, that is the best scenario—stay with your loved ones. I believe that is more common in other cultures than it is in ours anymore. Getting a good attorney who specializes in the problems seniors face will save you a lot of heartache.

Here I want to warn you that pride is a poor bedfellow. If you find yourself in financial straits and can't afford the necessities of life, there are many resources out there. There is no excuse for going hungry. Find the local food bank; that is what they are there for. Look for the local group called the gleaners, who have lots of food available that even goes to waste because there aren't enough people to take it. Call Meals on Wheels or your local senior center or the senior care hotlines, who will point you in the right direction.

I know of one man who is destitute and too proud to ask for help. We found that he lives on one very small meal per day, because that is all he can afford. I think all of us know how some people ate dog food because it used to be cheaper than people food. This is terrible, but it does exist. There is so much help out there, even food being wasted. There is no excuse to go hungry in most cities. *Pride is a poor substitute for a hot meal.* Don't let pride block the care you need. You have spent your life working and caring for others; you paid for that care through the years of paying Social Security taxes, etc. Regardless of Obama claiming that we think we are entitled to it, you *are* entitled to it. You paid for that insurance all your working life.

If you have had a control freak for a spouse who wouldn't let you handle any of the finances and may have kept all your friends and family away, then when they pass, you will need help. Go to the bank, and they will teach you how to balance your bank account. You can also go to a senior center or government department for care of the elderly and they will help you establish a budget and guide you handling the regular living tasks.

You will become very vulnerable to the TV and Internet ads. You finally got hold of some money you can control, so now you have a feeling of empowerment and will tend to buy, buy, buy. The commercials all sound *so* good and will cure what ails you. Be careful—like the old cure-all snake oil in a bottle, it usually doesn't work.

Now that you have control of your life and finances, you will feel lost for a while, but the best thing you can do is get involved with the groups in your church or local senior center affairs. This will get you out and help you develop social skills. You need to make friends, so get out and volunteer somewhere. Nurture friendships. You need them now more than ever. They can also be a real source of guidance in running your own life.